Mothman

AND OTHER CURIOUS ENCOUNTERS

OTHER BOOKS BY LOREN COLEMAN
Tom Slick: True Life Encounters in Cryptozoology

Mysterious America: The Revised Edition

Cryptozoology A to Z: The Encyclopedia of Loch Monsters, Sasquatch, Chupacabras, and Other Authentic Mysteries of Nature (with Jerome Clark)

The Field Guide to Bigfoot, Yeti, and Other Mystery Primates Worldwide (with Patrick Huyghe)

Creating Kinship (with Sharon Kaplan Roszia and Annette Baran)

Working With Rural Youth (with Dan Porter)

Tom Slick and the Search for the Yeti

Working with Older Adoptees (with Karen Tilbor, Helaine Hornby and Carol Boggis)

Suicide Clusters

Unattended Children (with Susan Partridge and Roy Partridge)

Curious Encounters

Mysterious America

Creatures of the Outer Edge (with Jerome Clark)

The Unidentified (with Jerome Clark)

Mothman

AND OTHER CURIOUS ENCOUNTERS

by LOREN COLEMAN

PARAVIEW PRESS

NEW YORK

On that bleak day, December 15, 1967, sixty-seven fell.
Forty-six were gone forever.
This book is dedicated to the victims of the Silver Bridge disaster,
the families, and the loved ones they left behind.
And the unnamed heroes who saved twenty-one.
Tragedies so enormous live evermore.

Contents

Introduction:
The News Coming In

The wire service ticker was spitting out the bulletin…

> Location: Point Pleasant, West Virginia
> Dateline: November 15, 1966
> Two young couples reported to Mason County sheriff's department tonight they have had a curious encounter with a monster.
> "It was shaped like a man, but bigger. Maybe six and a half or seven feet tall. And it had big wings folded on its back," eyewitness Roger Scarberry told Deputy Millard Halstead.
> Roger's wife, Linda finished his thought: "But it was those eyes that got us. It had two big red eyes, like automobile reflectors."
> The Scarberrys and another couple, Steve and Mary Mallete, had seen something strange at the abandoned World War II ammunition dump, known locally as the TNT area.
> "For a minute we could only stare at it. Then it just turned and sort of shuffled towards the open door of the old power plant. We didn't wait around." Roger continued.

Thus began America's first notice of a series of sightings of a strange *something* that would be quickly named "Mothman." A month after the publicity began, a journalist innocently showed up in town to live among the locals, hoping to understand what was happening.

During the next thirteen months, he would make five trips to Point Pleasant, staying for many weeks scrutinizing the case. The investigator's name is John A. Keel. His experiences appeared in a series of articles and in his book on the subject, *The Mothman Prophecies*.

Keel has been linked forever with Mothman, and he even told me recently that people can't think of him without thinking of Mothman, although his life is much more diverse than this single group of reports. This "typecasting" will continue, as a fictional contemporary version of John Keel appears as reporter John Klein, played by Richard Gere, in the new major motion picture from Screen Gems, also starring Laura Linney, Will Patton, Debra Messing, and directed by Mark Pellington.

The impact and timing of Mothman-related events continues to amaze. Take for example, David Grabias' plans to interview John Keel in Point Pleasant for his 2002 documentary on Mothman. They were to fly Keel from his Manhattan home to West Virginia, to do the taping. But Keel never made it. His flight was cancelled. The date he was to fly to Mothman country—September 11, 2001.

Keel's book and Pellington's movie help us move these events into context. But how can we understand them? How can we fit this entity into human consciousness, let alone *Homo sapiens'* history and experience? Perhaps we should merely throw aside this weird wonder as a hoax, a lover's lane illusion, a misidentification, and go on with our lives. But we can't. The incidents in West Virginia, we begin to discover, do not live in a vacuum. As you will learn in this book, Mothman may have more to tell us than we could have ever imagined.

More about Mothman later, but first let's put some of this weirdness in perspective and examine some of Mothman's precursors.

The Fortean Milieu

Charles Fort, the early 20th century author and intellectual, skeptically viewed the "final" answers that modern Science had given for odd bits of data he found in its own official journals as only an indication of the silliness of blind faith. Today, to scrutinize the world the way Fort did is rather common, as questioning authority, critically looking at experts and governments, is in vogue. But being "Fortean," in many ways, seems like a recent human development. Do not, however, confuse the Fortean view with an exercise in gullibility or "believing" in anything that comes along, as some debunkers who call themselves "skeptics" would have you feel. Indeed, Forteans, as real skeptics, do not accept as true, uncritically, anything. Instead, sensing that "belief" is the realm of religion, Forteans remain open-minded to all evidence, pro or con, in an effort at a deeper understanding. This book's exploration of Mothman and related curious encounters will examine the underlying patterns, the oneness that shines through many weird moments along the way. They, nevertheless, are enigmas enmeshed in mysteries, and our minds have a hard time wrapping themselves around them.

At what seems like the edge of the fringe, with the most bizarre of the strange, one such story illustrates a couple points. In April 1966, sixteen-year-old Kathy Reeves of Newport, Oregon saw three tiny tree stumps walking across a meadow near her home. Well, now, that would seem unusual, in and of itself. She noted these "walking stumps" were orange, blue, white, yellow, and watermelon-colored. Soon a torrent of oddities broke loose around her hometown. UFOs were sighted. Newport residents started talking about how nearby Pioneer Mountain had always been weird. A local couple told officials they had seen a group of staring Cyclops. The Reeves family, who actually lived on the side of Pioneer Mountain, started experiencing waves of poltergeist activity. Objects in their home danced about and globes of bluish light bounced along their roof. Finally, the Reeves family did what most sane people have done in such situations; they moved.

This Oregon case fits the Fortean (which is often incorrectly labeled "paranormal" by debunkers, bookstores, and libraries) milieu, and somewhat also the UFO world, for a number of reasons. The series of events are called a "flap," an old Air Force term that has been applied to flying saucer and related accounts where there is a defined series of incidents in a limited period of time. The location is a special "spooky site"—a window area with a specific haunted history. The area, Newport, Oregon, serves, if you will, as a "new port" for the phenomena. Once the manifestations began, it was as if the floodgates had opened. We see this again and again in such window areas as Pioneer Mountain. So many people shared the sightings that the events have drifted nicely into the lore of weird places.

Furthermore, the witnesses' name, Reeves, is among those special family titles that have been pinpointed as playing a magnetic role in the "name game." John Keel once told me that people named Reeve/Reeves have a lot of strange experiences. Many monster witnesses have been named Reeves. A glance at the indexes of *Fortean Times* will show a sprinkling of Reeves and Reeve, as witnesses and contributors. A man named Reeves was the primary witness in a now famous Brooksville, Florida UFO case. As Jerome Clark has written: "A man so obscure as to be barely known to most other residents of the rural area where he lived, John F. Reeves, 66, became the focus of international attention in 1965, when he reported an encounter with a UFO and its occupant." Contactees Bryant and Helen Reeve reached celebrity status in the 1950s after writing their book, *Flying Saucer Pilgrimage.* Much has been written of the tragic coincidences whirling around the lives of the actors (George Reeves and Christopher Reeve) who played the television and movie *Superman* (a fictional character who was an alien come to Earth to assist humans) and the "superman" (Keanu Reeves) in *The Matrix.* There is a reason it's called the Name Game.

The Damned and the Undamned

By naming various aspects of the phenomena like this, the question arises: Has the field of the unexplained become a series of conventionalizations itself? Frankly, we have to come to grips with the concept that it's really weird out there. And it's a lot weirder than it was yesterday. By now almost everyone has heard of UFOs, poltergeists, Nessie, Bigfoot, Champ, and even the Jersey Devil. But is there an exclusion of the most bizarre even from the likes of ufology (the study of UFOs) and cryptozoology (the study of hidden or unknown animals)? Has there been a discrimination against taking Mothman seriously? There seems to be an elaborately strange slew of entities and locations haunting the countryside. Even researchers into matters cryptozoological, psychic, or otherwise strange, have been taken aback by the vast waves of critters, experiences, and places that just do not fit into the usual world of the explained.

One old story serves as a quick illustration. Scientists did not accept meteorites, literally stones from the skies, as real for centuries. As Charles Fort, the modern founder of unexplained phenomena investigations, points out in his *The Book of the Damned*, it hasn't been long since experts were trying to convince people that the stones from the skies were either the result of "volcanic activity or whirlwinds." Falling stones were very simply "damned," i.e. not accepted by science. Now, of course, they are "undamned" and found in museums and textbooks. Earthquake lights, once a strictly Fortean phenomena—one that Fort chronicled and championed in his books, are creeping into some geological textbooks. Cryptozoologically speaking, sea serpents have attained a sort of quasi-acceptance among some biologists and zoologists; they are well on their way to becoming "meteorites." In the following pages are creatures which appear to border on myth, but which may one day be proven to be more than folklore. Mostly what we are hearing from eyewitnesses and then tracking down is that there are things and sites more bizarre than even an investigator of the unknown can possibly imagine.

Take Bigfoot. These hairy, eight-foot, man-like beasts were little heard of outside the Pacific Northwest before the work of John Green, Rene Dahinden, and Ivan Sanderson brought them to the attention of the reading public in the 1950s. By now, however, people have pigeonholed Bigfoot into a nice comfortable category, monsterwise, and have been less than enthusiastic about recognizing other large hairy beasts that happened to turn up here and there. But they are popping up, in and out of places once neglected in studies of hairy hominids. In Pennsylvania, folks are seeing upright hairy things that look like werewolves. A few years ago, near York, Nebraska, a local resident saw a satyr, a living, breathing Pan-like, goat-footed beastie. People around a village in Georgia recently saw a peg-legged Bigfoot. And around the Great Lakes, researchers like Mark A. Hall have gathered together an interesting bunch of reports of three-toed anthropoids; Ken Coon had gathered similar accounts from southern California. Even the Loch Ness Monster seems tame by comparison nowadays. Off Virginia in the Potomac, a huge snake-like monster, "Chessie," has been routinely seen most summers since over thirty people saw "it" in 1978. And some of these witnesses are, we are told, Central Intelligence Agency employees. Down along the Swanee River in Florida, a long-necked, gill-mouthed creature nicknamed "Pinkie" became all the rage a few years ago.

Throughout the book, I will introduce you to the truly bizarre. Encounters with giant winged Mothman of Appalachia and strange reptilian Lizardmen of the swampy Ohio River Valley. Researchers may sense they have to go to the Congo to hunt cryptids (unknown animals) that seem to resemble dinosaurs, but from my trekking around the backroads and woods, interviewing hundreds of witnesses, and reading the cases investigated by other dedicated researchers, some pretty strange stuff is to be found right in our own backyards.

More Curious Encounters On the Road Again

In *Mysterious America*, I examined the phantasmagoria of black panthers, kangaroos, phantom clowns, alligators-in-the-sewers, mad gassers, and other anomalies a bit beyond the experiences of your everyday trek to the corner store. I continue that journey in this book. Along the way, you'll learn of extraordinary encounters by ordinary people at some of the spookiest spots on the horizon. The world is mighty weird, and together we will experience some of its wonders.

Charles Fort once noted that the excluded and damned data "arrange themselves in mass-formations that pass and pass and keep on passing." We shall see that this Forteana, as it is now called in his honor (or his humorous dishonor, he might think), is not easy to place into neat little boxes. It's like trying to pour water in a bucket full of holes; you pour it in and before you know it, it's someplace else. Forteana is like that.

Don't be frustrated by the usual lack of nice, neat explanations for this collection of sightings, stories, reports, and tales. Forteans are often happy to gather the information together and present the data for data's sake. But looking at the patterns is enjoyable too, for in deciphering the underlying oneness, perhaps we can get a hint of the deeper process. Or at least as humans, that is the fiction we carry around in our heads.

Lifting the Curtain

One thing that gets in the way of any openness to the earnest insights available from this damned data is the foggy curtain of ridicule that obscures the view. Many observers who have unique encounters often experience ridicule when they tell their stories. In 1953, J. Allen Hynek, the astronomer-turned-UFO-researcher, noted that "ridicule is not part of the scientific method, and the public should not be taught that it is." Nevertheless, despite calls for critical thinking, scientists and others ignore Mothman by simply making fun of it without "looking" at it. This "ridicule curtain"—as Hynek first called it in reference to UFO sightings and which I appropriate and apply more broadly here—exists to deter witnesses from coming forth, as the societal status quo calls for normalcy, not out-of-the-ordinary encounters.

Nevertheless, what often happens is that as such sightings start to come in, the ridicule curtain begins to lift, ever so carefully. Often, as the encounters of prior witnesses are revealed, the ridicule curtain may not be a major limiting factor for a few days or months. But for the equilibrium of the establishment, various methods are used (e.g. the dismissing explanation, the seven day wonder put down, the silly season rationale, the escaped animal explanation) to regain the non-threatening environment in which Mothman and monsters do not exist. In some ways, without dwelling on this social situation but on the data, our Fortean task is to deal with the chronicles and look for patterns.

As you will soon discover, I have tried to point out some interesting archetypes that seem to be at the nucleus of these stories. It's an amusing game, harmless, and done in good humor. Maybe a member of officialdom will come up with a nice lateral thinking explanation that shall satisfactorily quiet the questions raised by these nasty bits of data. Nonetheless, the reports will remain, just the same. The Fortean procession of the damned will continue. The circle, which one can start measuring anywhere, remains unbroken.

So now, let's get out on the road again.

CHAPTER 1

Flatwoods

It looked worse than Frankenstein.
It couldn't have been human.—KATHLEEN MAY

The smell was like oil on hot metal. You know, that greasy, sweet, slippery odor, slightly burnt and perhaps even appealing. But then more and more of it seemed to be saturating the molecules all around. It filled your nose. It permeated your pores. It made you sick to your stomach. It wouldn't go away. The creepy feeling was close, something beyond the knowing, beyond understanding.

The dog was sick; the boys ran down the hill and vomited. In two days, the dog was dead, and no one thereabouts would ever be the same.

It all began innocently enough. The autumn air clued in the kids to what they might want to do that day. How about a friendly pickup game of football, they asked each other? The date was September 12, 1952. The place, Flatwoods, West Virginia.

Weird West Virginia

West Virginia has always had an aura about it, even before it was a state. Colonists mumbled that American Indians avoided the area because the "devil" haunted the region. Certainly if any myth-making existed in such a statement, it was helped along by the fact that Lewis Wetzel who was born in what is today West Virginia killed every Indian he could and drove others westward from the countryside. Having a very dark complexion, wild black eyes, extremely broad shoulders, an expansive chest, and muscular arms and legs, Wetzel was a striking man, even if only five feet ten inches tall. His hair was raven and lavish, reaching below his knees. It is said he grew his hair so long so as to be a superior scalp for any Indian. Perhaps it is fitting that he is buried at the spooky spot that is Moundsville. Today his ethnic cleansing would not be tolerated, and modern analysts would classify him as a serial killer. But few think of that as they travel through today's Wetzel County on their way to our first stop in weird West Virginia.

Centered in the middle of the state, with Wetzel County north, Mason to the West, Fayette to the south, and Webster next door to the East, the 513 square miles of Braxton County are some of the most rural of the state. The county has been a focal area of strange incidents, and there are even signposts to acknowledge it nowadays. Highway markers at the town limits read "Flatwoods, Home of the Flatwoods Monster." A few local people remain who remember the night a "Monster" landed.

The Thing on the Hill

On the evening of that September 12th, as it grew dark, lights began flashing across the sky. Around the same time, four local boys were playing football, when they saw what they said was a "shooting star" fall to earth on the top of the hill adjacent to the playground, on the ole Bailey Fisher property. Actually, they said it had just gone around the corner of the hill. With the curiosity that kids had during the 1950s, they decided to check it out. On the way up the hill, they yelled out their excitement at the Kathleen May home. One of the boys, Ronald Shaver shouted: "A flying saucer has landed on the hill and we are going to look at it." Mrs. May, along with her two sons, accompanied the group up the hill, with Tommy Hyer joining them along the way.

Here in the foothills of Appalachia, going up the incline, over 850 yards to the crest of the ridge, was no easy task. When the group, Eugene Lemon, 17, Neal Nunley, 14, Mrs. May, her sons Eddie, 13, and Teddie, 14, Ronald Shaver, 10, Teddie Neal, 10, and Tommy Hyer, 10, reached the top, they immediately noticed the smell, sighted the rolling unnatural fog, and saw a strange bright light ahead. Their eyes began to water. Lemon's big old dog had run ahead, barking out a racket. The thing on the hill was glowing and hissing, ten feet long, and appeared to have a solid enough form, from their vantage point about 100 yards away. Following the path on the Bailey Fisher property that lead to the light, the group proceeded slowly but steadily. All of a sudden, Lemon's dog streaked back by, tongue out and tail between its legs. British zoologist/reporter Ivan T. Sanderson, who went on assignment to Flatwoods immediately after the incident, picks up the story from there:

As they rounded the last bend, Mrs. May called out to Eugene Lemon that she saw a pair of eyes in an oak tree to the left ahead, saying there was either an opossum or a raccoon in the tree. She asked Neal Nunley, who said that he was carrying the torch, to flash it in that direction. When he did so, its light disclosed what one and all affirm—despite any published reports to the contrary—answers to the following description. Each person added individual details, but the group was never in conflict.

The entity's top was level with a branch of the tree, and it seemed to end about some six feet below. It was about the size of an enormous man down to the waist. It did not have any arms or anything else sticking out of it, but it had a distinct "head." This was shaped like an "ace of spades" (they all repeated this). However, this "head" had a large circular window in it through which they could see (a) "darkness" and (b) two "things like eyes, which stayed fixed and shone straight out." When further questioned about the latter, the witnesses agreed that these were two objects behind a translucent panel, that emitted light, pale blue in color, in the form of direct, fixed beams of about the dimensions of a standard three-cell flashlight. These, they all said, were focused way above their heads and to the south, and only moved with the entity as it began to glide around. This it finally did, first toward them, and then in the direction of an object which was still lying pulsing in the tall grass nearby.

As the creature seemed to float on air toward them, the group all ran from the hill back to the May home to call the sheriff. As John Keel noted when he talked about the case: "Eugene Lemon did the rational thing. He' fainted dead away...Lemon's dog was stretched out at the foot of the hill, vomiting."

Grabbing the limp boy, the group took off in a dead run trying to distance themselves from the creature. Although the entity did not follow the group, all of them ran for their lives—doing something the dog had done much earlier. Little Tommy Hyer would later tell Ivan T. Sanderson, that he crawled under the fence in the field to get away, but that Kathleen cleared the six foot gate without opening it.

The sheriff, Robert Carr, and deputy Burnell Long, were investigating a report of a burning object thought to be a downed airplane, below Gassaway on the Elk River, near Sugar Creek. By the time they got to the Flatwoods scene, people who had heard the story and had gone to see the "Monster" for themselves had unintentionally destroyed much of the evidence. Nevertheless, Sheriff Carr, and later West Virginia UFO investigator Gary Barker, Sanderson, and others found gummy residue in the area, but were not overly concerned by this substance. Sanderson felt some of the smell and sticky substance on vegetation might have been from a special type of grass in the area, "tar-grass." Researchers would sense the vomiting and fainting that did occur after the sighting were purely from fright. Recently, in discussing the Flatwoods case, however, John Keel asked, if there was nothing to the horrible toxic smell, why then did the dog die? Keel recommended that if the grave of that dog could ever be found, perhaps modern DNA tests could unlock the mystery of what had killed this dog.

Little Owls, Giant Owls, and Aliens

What was the Flatwoods UFO Monster? Those with ideas of what it was have spanned a wide horizon. Gary Barker was interested in viewing the entity as a visitor from outer space. In 2000, debunker Joe Nickell, in *The Skeptic* magazine, has been very critical of the incident, and how others have reported it. For example, Nickell wrote: "Recent accounts have garbled details, with Brookesmith (1995), for example, incorrectly reporting five of the children as belonging to Mrs. May, and Ritchie (1994) referring to the monster's hoodlike feature as a 'halo,' which he compared with those in Japanese Buddhist art." But it is Nickell who has attempted to diminish the incident the most.

As Nickell writes: "There remains to be explained 'the Flatwoods Monster,' a.k.a. 'the Phantom of Flatwoods,' 'the Braxton County Monster,' 'the Visitor from Outer Space,' and other appellations…I agree with most previous investigators that the monster sighting was not a hoax….Clearly, something they saw frightened them, but what?"

Nickell reached back to a comment retired Air Force major Donald Keyhoe had made in 1953, when he reported that locals had concluded the "monster" was probably "a large owl perched on a limb" with underbrush beneath it having "given the impression of a giant figure" and the excited witnesses having "imagined the rest."

"I believe," Nickell writes, "this generic solution is correct, but that the owl was not from the family of 'typical owls' (Strigidae, which includes the familiar great horned owl) but the other family (Tytonidae) which comprises the barn owls. Several elements in the witnesses' descriptions help identify the Flatwoods creature specifically as *Tyto alba*, the common barn owl, known almost worldwide….Considering all of the characteristics of the described monster, and making small allowances for misperceptions and other distorting factors, we may conclude (adapting an old adage) that if it looked like a barn owl, acted like a barn owl, and hissed, then it was most likely a barn owl."

Fortean author and cryptozoologist Mark A. Hall, however, noted in 2001 that Nickell never correctly mentions how big the Flatwoods Monster was reported to be. Estimates from the witnesses ranged from six feet for just the body of the floating monster to ten feet if it was measured from the ground to the top of its cape. But Nickell's reconstructive drawing shows a monster of half that height compared with an owl. As Hall writes: "That would mean an owl three feel tall at the lowest estimate and five feet tall for a standing monster. They don't get that big. The barn owl measures only in a range of fourteen to twenty inches from bill to tail."

Mark Hall makes the point that this creature might have more to do with flying saucers, or aliens from other globes of lights which landed elsewhere in Braxton County that night, than it has to do with giant owls.

Braxton Invaders

Indeed, there were others who saw things that night and the next. A Birch River resident claimed to have seen a bright orange object circling the Flatwoods area. James Knob, a location, not a person's name, was said to have been hit by one. Some kind of glowing light came down near Sugar Creek. Remember the "crashed airplane" the sheriff was investigating that night? Woodrow Eagle who called the sheriff in Sutton had reported that crash. There are rumors that a woman and her mother came forward and said that they had seen the same creature at a spot eleven miles away.

Mark Hall has discovered another piece of the puzzle in professor James Gay Jones' *Appalachian Ghost Stories and Other Tales*. Jones relates that on September 12th, the same night as the Flatwoods encounter, two eyewitnesses, George and Edith Snitowsky of New York, were driving on the road between Gassaway and Frametown, West Virginia, just north of an oddly named place—Strange Creek. Their car, equipped with a brand new battery, stalled, mirroring what happens when a UFO is around and disrupts the electromagnetic system of the automobile. A nauseating smell then made their baby gag. George got out of the car and searched for what smelled so badly. Looking down the slope of the highway, he saw a large globe moving slowly back and forth, hovering over the ground, and giving off a soft, violet light. George moved closer and felt the "sensation of thousands of needle-like vibrations" on his skin. Then he got sick and staggered back to the car.

Edith Snitowsky screamed, and yelled that something was behind him. He turned to see "a figure about eight or nine feet tall with a big head, bloated body, and long, spindly arms gliding rapidly" toward him.

The couple, safely inside the car, locked it quickly. Terrified, they watched as one of those long, spindly arms stretched across their windshield. The end was forked. Creepy, indeed. The couple crouched in horror. When George looked up, he saw the monster gliding away.

Waiting and waiting, finally they saw a glowing globe, swaying back and forth, lift above the trees, and take off into the sky, leaving a light trail.

They found a motel in Sutton, tried to sleep, and were startled the next morning when a gas station attendant showed them a V-burnt brown spot on their hood.

Though John A. Keel, in *The Eighth Tower*, briefly mentioned this encounter occurred on September 13, 1952, not the 12th, and spells the witnesses' name, Snitowski, with an "i" not a "y," clearly the Flatwoods-Sugar Creek-Frametown incidents did occur. Even debunkers admit that. What happened in West Virginia that night in September, with several UFOs landing all over the rural countryside and unloading weird creatures, almost seems like a scene from *War of the Worlds*. But it really happened in 1952. Perhaps it was the first wave, before Mothman "visited" Point Pleasant. But exactly what the entities were, or what their purpose was in Braxton County, remains a mystery.

Bakery Trucks and Balls of Fire

A mere eight years later, Braxton County was involved in what John Keel calls today a "classic" monster case. It began around 11:00 PM on Friday, December 30, 1960, when, Charles Stover, driving a bakery truck, rounded a curve on a deserted, backwoods road near Hickory Flats, West Virginia, between Braxton and Webster Counties. Like the Sugar Creek witnesses, Stover almost hit a monster, which stood upright, hair all over its body. Pulling his truck to a sharp stop, Stover looked back to see a six foot tall, human-shaped, hairy figure right next to the road, staring at him. Being a little scared, he stepped on the gas, and raced along until he reached a truck stop where he related his story to a group of men. They immediately armed themselves and went to the spot where they found strange marks on the ground. They also noticed that large rocks had been overturned by *something*. But they couldn't find any trace of the monster.

West Virginia, in general, was in the middle of a flap in 1960. Besides the Braxton County creature of December 30th, several significant Monongahela Forest encounters happened that summer. In one extraordinary incident, W. C. "Doc" Priestly was driving near Marlington, about 55 miles southeast of Flatwoods, when his car malfunctioned and stalled. All of a sudden, next to the road, Priestly saw a giant hominid creature with all of its long hair standing on end. His companions, ahead of him, became worried, and backed up their bus. When this happened, the beast's hairs dropped down and it disappeared into the forest. Priestly's car started up again, and he drove along. The thing then appeared again at the side of the road. And again, his friends came back to find Priestly, and the creature vanished for the last time into the trees.

In another summer 1960 incident, this one near Davis, 75 miles northeast of the Priestly encounter, at the extreme northern end of the Monongahela Forest, a group of campers saw a "horrible monster." The witnesses said it "had two huge eyes that shone like big balls of fire …. It stood every bit of eight feet tall and had shaggy long hair all over the body." The creature shuffled off into the night, and the campers packed up the next morning as quickly as they could. Around the same time, according to Fortean researcher John Lutz, when he was working at WFBR Radio, he and his boss, Lou Corbin, investigated the Pocahontas County "Apple Devil," a creature that would take bites out of apples in the orchards around the town of Marlington.

Meanwhile, an eight-foot-tall Bigfoot-type creature with "balls-of-fire" eyes was seen by many people, around Parsons, also in the northern part of the Monongahela Forest during that weird summer of 1960.

Five years later, 30 miles northwest of Davis, just outside of the Monongahela Forest, a secluded area near the Tygart River at Grafton was the scene of a series of creature sightings. In 1995, Mark A. Hall discovered, while digging into the Gray Barker Collection in West Virginia, the unpublished details of what was called locally the "Grafton Monster." Robert Cockrell, a newsman at the Grafton *Sentinel*, first spied the creature around 11 PM, on June 16, 1965. Cockrell was motoring along Riverside Drive, on the wild west side of Grafton, when he came around a wide curve. He told interviewer Gray Barker: "I know the road well, the night was clear…As I glanced up, my high beams picked up a huge white obstruction on the right side of the road standing between the road and the river bank on a cleared off section of grass. After glimpsing the Thing, I speeded up to get off that road as soon as possible. My impressions of the beast were: It was between seven and nine feet tall, it was approximately four feet wide, and has a seal like skin or covering which had a sheen to it. It had no discernible head and did not move as I passed by." Cockrell returned with the police to no avail. Others reported seeing it after his sighting, and Cockrell wrote up two articles that were highly censored by the paper's editor. And then it disappeared into the monster lore of West Virginia.

The headlessness of this Grafton Monster, the balls-of-fire eyes of the Monongahela creatures, and the glowing eyes and cape-like "ace-of-spades halo" of the Flatwoods Monster serve as weird elements foreshadowing what people would describe when confronted with Mothman during 1966-1967. The ingredient of wings, of course, is another matter.

CHAPTER 2

Winged Weirdies

Since humans first looked toward the skies, people have been seeing a wild assortment of flying creatures, creatures so bizarre that they should only exist in the privacy of someone's nightmares. But the fact remains that eyewitnesses have reported seeing very real winged weirdies for centuries.

Sky Serpents

How are we to file away or understand reports of sky serpents, the things that were seen in the air before airplanes and UFOs flew about? Take the Bonham, Texas, *Enterprise,* story which noted that during June 1873, a local resident "saw something resembling an enormous serpent" floating above his farm. Others working nearby saw it too and were understandably unnerved. "It seemed to be as large and long as a tele-graph pole, (and) was of a yellow striped color." The men could see the serpent "coil itself up, turn over, and thrust forward its huge head as if striking at some thing."

Shortly thereafter, according to the *New York Times* of July 7, 1873, a similar phenomenon appeared over Fort Scott, Kansas, "halfway above the horizon." Witnesses stated, "a huge serpent, apparently perfect in form, was plainly seen."

Charles Fort notes that a sky serpent "flap" took place in Darlington County, South Carolina, in May 1888. This time the thing supposedly made a "hissing sound." But there are other reports with which Fort was unfamiliar. On December 5, 1762, a "twisting serpent" lit up the English town of Bideford, Devon, for six minutes before fading away, and a "ser-pent of fire" taking the form of a horseshoe passed over Geneva on May 15, 1811. It was also seen in Paris. In more modern times, March 1935, something described as "a large shining form resembling a gigantic snake wriggling forth in the northwestern sky" appeared over southern Norway and Denmark. It is said to have had four or five curves and to have moved in a vertical position with its "head" pointed toward the earth. Back in the Americas, a similar object was observed twice over Cruz Alta, Brazil, in December of the same year. When it reappeared in July 1937 its "head" had become a ball of fire.

Then there was the Great Scare of 1857-1858, when in the late dusk a giant serpent hovered above a steamboat slowing for a landing along the Missouri River in Nebraska. It seemed to be breathing fire, say accounts, and it had "lighted streaks" along its sides.

Sightings must have continued, for some years later a song passed into local folk tradition:

'Twas a dark night in Sixty~six
When we was layin' steel
We seen a flyin' engine come
Without no wing or wheel
It came a-roarin' in the sky
With lights along the side.
And scales like a serpent's hide.

By the turn of the century Nebraskans were no longer confusing serpents and UFOs. In February 1897, the mystery "airships" had begun flying over the state, and in the years ahead stories were revived of a giant creature in the waters of Alkali Lake near Hay Springs (first told by the Native Americans to the first white settlers in the area). One observer said, "its head was like an oil barrel, shiny black in the moonlight. Its flashing green eyes were spitting fire." With these incidents, we are moving into new and uncharted territory, where the line between "machines" and "animals" becomes blurred, as, indeed, does the line that divides the various types of Fortean phenomena.

For example, reports of weird aerial constructions like one seen near Copiapo, Chile in 1868 and cited by Charles Fort from *Zoologist* for July of the same year just do not make much sense. The object carried lights and was driven by a noisy motor; a contemporary source described it as "a gigantic bird; eyes wide open and shining like burning coals; covered with immense scales, which clashed together with a metallic sound."

Almost a hundred years later, near Point Pleasant, West Virginia, John A. Keel would investigate the reports of a giant bird-like creature named Mothman and comment on its uncanny ability to fly about without flapping its wings. Keel felt something more mechanical than monstrous was about. Perhaps.

America's Birdmen of Yesteryears

Birdmen reports in America start in earnest with the report from W. H. Smith published in the *New York Sun* on September 18, 1877. The sightings concerned a "winged human form" flying over Coney Island, Brooklyn, New York.

A few years later we find an analogous story in the July 29, 1880 issue of the *Louisville* (Kentucky) *Courier-Journal*. The story reported that two local residents, C.A. Youngman and Ben Flexner, had seen what they at first took to be the wreck of a toy balloon in the sky the night before. But when the flying contraption came closer, the witnesses saw that it was really "a man surrounded by machinery which he seemed to be working with his hands." Wings or fins were protruding from his back, they reported, and the apparatus seemed to be propelled by their flapping. When the contraption began to descend, the flier would make the wings move faster and he would then ascend and continue flying along a horizontal path. Eventually he passed out of view and into the twilight.

But the Louisville flier wasn't the only object cavorting around the skies that summer in Kentucky. A family in Madisonville, a town located about a hundred miles to the southwest of Louisville, saw a peculiarly lighted object (certainly a very bizarre "unidentified flying object") moving southward that same evening. They reported that it changed shape and condensed from a circle into an oval, as it passed over the town's railway station.

A month and a half later, a similar but more grotesque man-bird was seen over New York. "One day last week," the *New York Times* announced to its readers on September 12th, "a marvelous apparition was seen near Coney Island. At the height of at least 1000 feet in the air a strange object was in the act of flying toward the New Jersey coast. It was apparently a man with bat's wings and improved frog's legs. The face of the man could be distinctly seen and it wore a cruel and determined expression. The movements made by the object closely resembled those of a frog in the act of swimming with his hind legs and flying with his front legs....When we add that his monster waved his wings in answer to the whistle of a locomotive and was of a deep black color, the alarming nature of the apparition can be imagined. The object was seen by many reputable persons and they all agree that it was a man engaged in flying toward New Jersey."

The creature apparently returned to the American skyways several years later. On April 16, 1897, a weird apparition sailed over Mount Vernon, Illinois. According to the *Saginaw Courier Herald*, more than a hundred people saw the gargoyle. "It was first observed about 8:30," reports the paper, "and continued in sight for half an hour. Mayor Wells, who had an excellent view of the mysterious visitor from the observatory attached to his residence, says it resembled the body of a huge man swimming through the air with an electric light on his back."

UFO investigator Gray Barker mentions in his *Book of Saucers* that he discovered an article in a 1922 edition of the Lincoln, Nebraska, *Daily Star* that quoted an eyewitness who had seen a large circular object land near his house and an eight-foot-tall being emerged from it. This is significant, for as John Keel has pointed out: "Dr. Jacques Vallee found a remarkably similar report from Nebraska in that same year, 1922, in a letter buried in the Air Force UFO files at Dayton, Ohio. The letter writer, William C. Lamb, was hunting near Hubbell, Nebraska; when, at 5:00 AM on Wednesday, February 22, 1922 he heard a high-pitched sound and saw a large, dark object pass overhead, blotting out the stars. He hid behind a tree, he said, and watched as the object landed. Next he saw 'a magnificent flying creature' which landed like an airplane and left tracks in the snow. It was at least eight feet tall. It passed by the tree where Lamb was hiding, and he tried to follow its tracks but never managed to catch up with it."

Flying Men in Flying Saucer Country

The North American public first became interested in the UFO mystery during the late 1940s when a virtual epidemic of flying saucers invaded our skies. And after Kenneth Arnold saw a group of metallic flying discs while making an informal reconnaissance flight on June 24, 1947, near Mt. Rainier, Washington, "saucer watching" became almost as popular a hobby for many people as bird watching. It wasn't long before the military, especially the U.S. Air Force, was drowning in UFO reports. But flying saucers weren't the only things people were seeing up in the skies during that time.

At least that's what Army officials at McChord Field in Washington state discovered when, in the early part of 1948, they were approached by sixty-one-year-old Mrs. Bernice Zaikowski, who had more than a conventional UFO sighting she wanted to talk about. She claimed that she had seen a man-bird from her backyard in nearby Chehalis, Washington.

"I know most people don't believe me," she told the officers, "but I have talked to some people in Chehalis that tell me they saw the man, too, and that he flew south from Chehalis and apparently came from the north or east."

As she spoke, Mrs. Zaikowski repeatedly emphasized that the creature she had seen was not a figment of her imagination. Other people had seen the man-bird, also, she kept telling the officials.

"It was about 3:00 PM on the Tuesday after New Year's Day (January 6, 1948), and there were a lot of small children coming home from school at the time," she reported to the McChord officials. "They saw the man, too, and asked me if they could go into my backyard so they could watch him longer as he flew toward the south end of the city."

Mrs. Zaikowski went on to say that she only went outside to see what the children were talking about when she heard "a sizzling and whizzing" sound coming from outdoors. When she went outside to trace the source of the sound she spotted the creature hovering about twenty feet above her barn. The flying weirdie seemed obviously to be a man but was equipped with long silver wings fastened over his shoulder with a strap. The figure hovered, banked, ascended, and then continued on his flight. He flew in an upright position and appeared to manipulate his wings by toying with controls strapped to his chest. The flier did not appear to be equipped with a propeller or any other source of motive power, added Mrs. Zaikowski.

Needless to say, the officials at McChord Field who interviewed Mrs. Zaikowski didn't know what to make of her report. "It sounds like one of those saucer deals," was the only comment the officials made. But, he also added, "I just can't put any stock in it at all."

And so ends the bizarre story of the Chehalis, Washington flying birdman. But just who was he? On the one hand, the creature appears to have been simply a man who had devised a new method of flying. For hundreds of years people have been attempting to fly with the aid of makeshift wings attached to the arms. Even the great Italian inventor and scholar, Leonardo da Vinci (1452-1519), played with the idea that man might be able to propel himself through the air by strapping artificial wings to his body. Could one man, who lived somewhere in rural Washington, have finally succeeded? While this is possible, it seems unlikely. Surely such an ingenious inventor would have patented his discovery, or at least would have been observed making many test flights. But the Chehalis flying man never made his discovery known, never sought to patent it, and apparently never told anyone about it. In fact, we don't really know what the Washington birdman was at all. Mrs. Zaikowski and the other witnesses who watched in astonishment as the birdman performed his aerial acrobatics saw something, but what it was, we may never know.

Whatever his nature, the birdman soon vanished. He was apparently never seen during January of 1948, over any towns neighboring Chehalis, which presumably lay in his flight path. He just disappeared as mysteriously as he had come. But this wasn't, of course, the first time in history that a birdman had winged his way over rural America. Nor was it to be the last in the Chehalis area.

In the Wake of Zaikowski's Encounter
By April of 1948 most of Washington's citizens had no doubt forgotten about Mrs. Zaikowski's claims. But our bizarre flying man had certainly

not put in his final appearance, even if no one was taking his existence very seriously. On April 9, 1948, two Longview, Washington state residents watched in amazement as the Washington birdman put on an encore performance. Mrs. Viola Johnson, a laundry worker, and James Pittman, a janitor, told newsmen that they had seen several of the bizarre fliers.

"They looked like three men in flying suits flying through the air." Mrs. Johnson reported. "They wore dark drab flying suits and as far as I can judge—I'm not very good at judging distance—they were 250 feet high, circling the city.

"They were going at about the same speed as a freight train and had some kind of apparatus on their sides which looked like guns but I know it couldn't have been guns. I couldn't see any propellers or any motors tied on them but I could hear motors which sounded like airplane motors, only not so loud.

"When they first came into sight I thought they looked like gulls but as they got closer I could see plainly that they were men. I couldn't make out their arms but I could see their feet dangling down and they kept moving their heads, like they were looking around. I couldn't tell if they had goggles on but their heads looked like they had helmets on. I couldn't see their faces."

Mrs. Johnson and Mr. Pittman soon called to some of their fellow laundry workers, who, unfortunately, arrived on the scene too late to witness the birdmen's performance. Nevertheless, several Longview residents did admit to reporters that they had heard sounds of airplane motors at the very time of the Johnson-Pittman sighting. Other witnesses in the area claimed that they had seen three aircraft circling high in the skies that day.

Meanwhile, Kenneth Arnold, who investigated some UFO sightings after his own flying saucer encounter, heard of two more flying men sightings from near Butte, Oregon, seen at dawn on September 16, 1948.

It seems another one of these creatures landed in a pecan tree right in the center of Houston, Texas. The incident occurred on July 18, 1953, while Mrs. Hilda Walker was standing outside her home at 2:30 in the morning. She was talking with a teenage girl at the time when they both spotted an odd "figure" flying toward them. As it came closer, these witnesses were able to see that the figure was actually a man with bat wings growing out of his back. The creature landed in Mrs. Walker's pecan tree, during which time the witnesses were able to get a better look at their otherworldly visitor. Mrs. Walker subsequently described him as "…a man with wings like a bat," dressed "in grey or black tight-fitting clothes." The figure was about six and a half feet tall and remained perched for about half a minute. A halo or "aura" seemed to radiate about him. The glow faded, reported the witnesses, and the batman gradually appeared to vanish into thin air.

John Keel writes of an account from an Arlington, Virginia, businessman who saw something in the company of three friends in the winter of 1968-69. In Prince William County, on a farm near Haymarket they investigated an unusual whoozing noise. Coming upon a dark figure over eight feet tall standing by a tree, the group retreated and turned on their automobile lights: "All we saw was this huge thing with large red-orange eyeballs and wing-like arms. We couldn't get out of there fast enough."

A World of Birdmen and Owlmen

These birdmen do not seem to be exclusively at home in the United States. Certainly there is a legacy dating back to Plato who wrote in the *Phaedrus* of a winged race of ancient men, and Homer who described the winged female Harpies. The Hindu culture of India tells of winged god-animals called *Garuda,* while in Thailand the *Garuda* is known as the "king of birds." Russia has a long tradition of what are called *Letayuschiy chelovek* ("flying human being"), with one of the more famous sightings happening on July 11, 1908, when explorer V. K. Arsenyev saw one near the mouth of the River Gobilli.

Europe also has had its share of winged weirdies, including some, it seems, that cavort around without heads. In the summer of 1915, for instance, four children in Cubeco, Portugal encountered an entity hovering in the air that looked to them very much like a headless "angel." They described it as "a figure like a statue made of snow which the rays of the sun had turned somewhat transparent." One of the witnesses,

Lucia Abobora later became one of the witnesses to the Blessed Virgin Mary-related flying disk seen at Fatima, Portugal, in 1917.

Four young people in Kent, England had an equally startling experience on the evening of November 16, 1963 as they walked home from a dance along a country road. Their report is particularly interesting, since their batman seems directly linked to an object which many might call a UFO.

The incident began innocently enough when a young man named John Flaxton (rhymes with Flatwoods' Braxton county), age 17, spotted what he first took to be a bright light in the sky. It had begun to descend by the time he called it to the attention of his companions. Soon, though, the object came down so low that it dipped behind some nearby trees. The teenagers panicked and started to run. The light then reappeared and floated about ten feet above the ground, following about 200 feet behind the running teenagers.

"It was bright gold and oval," one witness reported, "and when we moved it moved; when we stopped, it stopped."

The frightened teenagers were able to catch their breath a bit when the light vanished behind another clump of trees. But after several minutes of ominous silence, the witnesses heard twigs snapping. "Something" was obviously behind the trees and seemed to be stalking them. Then they saw it. "It" was a black, humanlike figure—up to a point. "But it didn't seem to have any head," one witness later told police. "There were huge wings on its back—like bat wings."

The already frightened group of youths ran full speed ahead after catching sight of the specter and didn't stop until they were a safe distance away from it.

Vietnam's Black Lady

These bizarre bird-creatures have also been seen in Asia. In Vietnam during the summer of 1969, three servicemen saw a female bat-winged creature, strikingly similar in appearance to the Houston batman, described earlier. The chief witness to this Asiatic version of batman was Earl Morrison. (Morrison is a step-nephew of Indiana researcher Don Worley, and it is through Worley's efforts that the details of the sighting finally reached publication, three years after the scary encounter.) Morrison, a private in the United States Marines, saw the thing while sitting atop a bunker near the city of Da Nang with two buddies. All three were just enjoying the warm evening air when suddenly, and for no apparent reason, they were compelled to look up into the sky. There they saw a glowing figure flying down toward them.

"We couldn't make out what it was at first," Morrison later told Don Worley. "It started coming towards us, really slowly. All of a sudden we saw what looked like wings, like a bat's, only it was gigantic compared to what a regular bat would be. After it got close enough so we could see what it was, it looked like a woman. A naked woman. She was black, everything was black. Her skin was black, her body was black, the wings were black, everything was black. But it glowed. It glowed in the night—kind of a greenish cast to it." The Houston batman, if you'll recall, was also black and glowed eerily before vanishing.

Morrison got a good look at the creature's wings. "We saw her arms towards the wings," he explained in his report, "and they looked like regular molded arms, each with a hand, and fingers, and everything, but they had skin from the wings going over them. And when she flapped her wings, there was no noise at first. It looked like her arms didn't have any bones in them because they were limber just like a bat."

The figure flew directly over the men at a height of about six or seven feet. The three servicemen just stared as it flew by, awestruck. Eventually they heard the flapping of wings before she gradually sailed out of sight.

A similar incident happened at Camp Okubo, Japan, in 1952. U.S. Air Force Private Sinclair Taylor reported that while on guard duty, he saw a flying seven-foot tall man with a wingspan of seven feet. When he fired at it repeatedly, it seemed to have hit the ground. But when he went looking for it, he found nothing there. Another soldier had a similar sighting a year later.

Birdmen of the Apocalypse
In a mysterious window-area called the Bridgewater Triangle in Massachusetts, I spent some time trekking to the site of a most dramatic

sighting of one of these birdmen, and interviewing the eyewitness. The encounter took place at 2 AM on a late summer's night in 1971. Norton, Massachusetts police sergeant Thomas Downy was driving along Winter Street in Mansfield toward his home in Easton. As he approached a place known, intriguingly, as "Bird Hill" in Easton at the edge of the Hockomock swamp, Downy was suddenly confronted by a huge winged creature over six feet tall with a wingspan of eight to twelve feet. As Sergeant Downy drew to a stop at the intersection, the bird flew straight up and, flapping its massive wings, disappeared over the dark trees into the swamp. Downy reported the sighting to the Easton police as soon as he reached home. A patrol car searched the area, but the huge bird was not sighted again. For weeks, his fellow officers called him "The Birdman," teasing him with the feathery name, but Downy stuck to his story. Downy was sincere and credible when I re-interviewed him and he guided me to Bird Hill, near some high power electricity lines in the Hockomock area. Oddly, Downy told me, he was struck by how the creature almost seemed to float upward, as much as flapping to get lift off.

In October 1974, near Elma, New York, Fortean investigator Virginia M. Miller reported that a witness saw an "immense birdlike creature with a wingspan of about nine or ten feet, a humanlike body and large grotesque head."

Some sort of birdman revisited England on Easter Sunday, April 17, 1976, when a similar creature was sighted in Cornwall by two girls, June and Vicky Melling, while on an outing during their vacation. They were sightseeing when they saw a "big feathered bird-man," as they described it, hovering over a church tower. They were so upset by their experience that they cut their vacation short and hastily returned home three days early.

The Cornwall birdman, which today is often called the "Owlman," was seen on at least three occasions after the Mellings' sighting. On July 3, 1976, two fourteen-year-old girls were camping among the trees near the same church where the Mellings had seen the creature. At about 10:00 PM they heard an odd "hissing" sound. (Note that Mrs. Zaikowski also heard a "sizzling" sound when she saw one of these creatures.) Then they saw a figure described "like a big owl with pointed ears, as big as a man." One of the witnesses, Sally Chapman said: "The eyes were red and glowing. At first, I thought it was someone dressed up, playing a joke, trying to scare us. I laughed at it, we both did, then it went up in the air and we both screamed. When it went up, you could see its feet were like pincers."

The other witness Barbara Perry added, "It's true. It was horrible, a nasty owl-face with big ears and big red eyes. It was covered in gray feathers. The claws on its feet were black. It just flew straight up and disappeared in the tree-tops."

The sighting lasted only a few seconds, but when the girls were separated and had to draw sketches of what they had seen, the drawings were remarkably similar. But Sally thought Barbara had "done the wings wrong." Sally depicted the wings as being more birdlike, whereas Barbara's illustration showed somewhat humanlike arms with feathers attached. Neither drawing precisely matched the one drawn of the Owlman of 1963, but the differences can perhaps be explained as the product of faulty observation caused by poor lighting conditions, the brevity of the sightings, and the extreme fright they evoked in the witnesses.

The next day three women saw the "Owlman" in almost the same spot. This letter from one witness, Jane Greenwood of Southport appeared in the *Falmouth Packet* for July 9, 1976:

> I am on holiday in Cornwall with my sister and our mother, I too have seen a big bird-thing like that pictured....It was Sunday (4th) morning and the place was in the trees near Mawnan Church, above the rocky beach. It was in the trees standing like a full-grown man, but the legs bent backwards like a bird's. It saw us and quickly jumped up and rose straight up through the trees. My sister and I saw it very clearly before it rose up. It has red slanting eyes and a very large mouth. The feathers are silver gray and so are his body and legs! The feet are like big black crab's claws. We were frightened at the time. It was so strange, like something out of a horror film. After the thing went up there were

crackling sounds in the tree-tops for ages. Our mother thinks we made it all up just because we read about these things, but that is not true. We really saw the birdman, though it could have been somebody playing a trick in very good costume and make-up. But how could it rise up like that? If we imagined it, then we both imagined the same thing at the same time.

Batsquatch

Washington State, since the 1948 sighting flap of the flying men, has been primarily the focus of reports of large hairy hominids, which have been tracked throughout the Pacific Northwest. These creatures are more generally called Bigfoot in California and Sasquatch in British Columbia, and thus referred by both names in Washington.

Not surprisingly, when the locals began talking about a remarkable winged creature near Washington's Mount Rainier, they saddled it with the moniker, Batsquatch.

The one and only Batsquatch sighting was reported on April 23, 1994, by an 18-year-old named Brian Canfield. He was driving his truck back to his isolated home, Camp One, in the foothills near Mt. Rainier (where, it should be noted, Kenneth Arnold saw the "first" flying saucers in 1947). Suddenly, the truck's engine shut down. Sitting in the middle of the highway, he watched in shock as a strange creature descended into his headlights' beams about ten yards ahead. The thing came down with a thump, and kicked up some dust. Canfield described the thing as a nine-foot-tall "Bigfoot-type creature," with blue-tinted fur, wings, tufted ears, bird-like claw feet, and a face like a wolf but without fangs, although its white teeth were very visible. The creature's eyes "were yellow and shaped like a piece of pie with pupils like a half-moon." C.R. Roberts, the columnist for the *Tacoma News Tribune* who interviewed Canfield, investigated his credibility and stated simply "I believe his story."

Canfield told Roberts, "It was standing there staring at me, like it was resting, like it didn't know what to think. I was scared. It raised the hair on me. I didn't feel threatened. I just felt out of place."

Next it unfolded its wings, which appeared as wide as the roadway, twitched its fingers, turned its head to look at Canfield, and started flapping its wings. Then an updraft shook Canfield's truck, as the Batsquatch flew away over the mountain. Soon thereafter, the truck engine kicked in and Canfield floored the vehicle to get home. Rushing in, Canfield's mother said, "His mouth was dry, he was pale, his hair was still standing on end." Reporter Roberts wrote: "I believe he saw something that night...I have no idea what he saw."

And, of course, neither does anyone else, except perhaps we may begin to find comfort in the fact that this creature fits nicely into the long history of winged weirdies. Through many centuries of authentic encounters, we now understand that the apex of such accounts exploded upon the American population in the essence of the Mothman of West Virginia.

CHAPTER 3

Mothman

You might have noticed by now that these birdmen, like UFOs, sometimes come in flaps. If it's seen once, it's likely to be seen again. That's certainly the lesson we learn from the owlmen of Cornwall and the Washington birdmen. It sometimes looks as though these creatures "inhabit" certain areas ("windows") for a short length of time before disappearing. In other words, these man-birds seem similar to the more conventional ghosts that people have been seeing in their homes for ages. Could these birdmen and batmen, then, be some sort of creatures that somehow become trapped in our world for short periods of time before finding an escape route back to their own universe? Or could they be cryptozoological specimens that actually live in these places but have never been caught and classified?

What we do know is that something seems to have happened in 1966 when one of these birdmen—or perhaps even a flock of them—suddenly started appearing all over the Ohio Valley in West Virginia, but especially near State Route 66, at Point Pleasant. From 1966 to 1967 this area was plagued by one of these creatures, which the local residents started dubbing "Mothman." The story of this Mothman "invasion" is a first-rate thriller, and all the more chilling since it is absolutely true, as many still-living witnesses will personally tell you. Luckily, these sightings were investigated by John Keel, a well-known investigator and author, and are chronicled in his book, *The Mothman Prophecies*. So we have an almost complete record of the appearances and disappearances of the elusive monster. John Keel told me in 2001 that he literally talked to hundreds of people who had seen this creature, but that he had only taken the cream of the crop to put in his book.

It's hard to determine just when the great Mothman epidemic first rocked the little community of Point Pleasant, West Virginia, one of those sleepy little towns where teenagers drag-race backward down Main Street on Saturday night when there isn't anything better to do–or spent time in local lover's lanes, as we shall see. We do know, though that Mothman was seen at least once before 1966. In 1961, one resident of the town was driving down Route 2 along the Ohio River with her father when she spotted this winged figure. She had just passed by a park when a tall figure suddenly appeared in the road ahead of her. It was a gray figure with folded wings across its back. Perhaps startled by the car, the creature unfolded its wings, which "practically filled the whole road," according to the witness, and then took off—straight up!

Hints of what was to come was foreshadowed on September 1, 1966, when several adults saw a man-shaped thing in the sky over Mississippi; on November 1st, when National Guardsman sighted a huge human-shaped object in a tree; and on November 12th, when a brown birdman flew over five men digging a grave at Clendrin, West Virginia.

However, Mothman only became a regular visitor to the Point Pleasant area in November 1966. This was during a time when many UFOs were flitting through West Virginia's skies as well.

TNT Area

Many of the Mothman sightings occurred in the countryside outside of the town itself. During World War II, explosives had been manufactured in Point Pleasant on the site of a former game preserve, which had been converted into a TNT dump. Over a hundred white bunkers were built for military purposes. The munitions plant was closed down after the war, and has been a wildlife preserve for many years. It is also the site for toxic waste, i.e. secretly discarded slag from a downriver atomic plant!

Today, the bunkers are still there, though in great disrepair. They are mostly deserted, though some are used for storage. A few bungalows and homes have also been built in the area. It's an eerie place, and it was here that Mothman apparently decided to stake out its nesting grounds.

West Virginia is a weird state, and this setting is one of the strangest around. Mason County, having one of those magical names with links to the mystical past of the Masonic traditions, seems a truly logical location for the 1966 series of Rt. 66 sightings. The TNT dump served as a hangout, a lovers' lane for young couples, teens, and twenty-somethings looking for some passion and necking, in those days. The location for the Mothman encounters seems natural.

The invasion began on the night of November 15th, when two young couples, Roger and Linda Scarberry, and Steve and Mary Mallette, were joyriding through the area late at night. They were passing through the maze of dirt roads that connect the bunkers and had just driven past an old generator plant when they spotted a huge figure lurking in the darkness at the side of the road.

Its two huge red eyes got their attention immediately. It terrified them. The figure was quite a sight. Linda Scarberry (who it must be noted is the former Linda McDaniel, an important detail as we will learn later on) subsequently explained to investigators that its eyes were blood red. The creature seemed totally oblivious to its earthly viewers, however, and merely walked toward the generator plant. But by this time the four witnesses really weren't interested in where the thing was headed. They just wanted to get out of there—and fast. Roger slammed on the gas and tried to maneuver his '57 Chevy out of the dump area as quickly as possible. But their mystery encounter was far from over. As they were speeding away, they saw the birdman standing on a hill by the side of the road. This second sighting revealed the most prominent detail of the manlike creature. It stood over six feet tall, its wings protruding from the center of its back, they said, "like an angel."

"It was shaped like a man, but bigger," explained Scarberry in his report on the hair-raising encounter. "Maybe six and a half or seven feet tall. And it had big wings folded against its back."

Its torso resembled a human being's except that it had no arms and its face was hard to distinguish, as if it was headless. It walked clumsily, like a penguin, and when it raised its wings to a 10-foot spread, it looked enormous. It then took off straight into the air, and headed right after the car.

"We were driving one hundred miles per hour," Roger later told investigators, "and that bird kept right up with us. It wasn't even flapping its wings." Yet it did make some sort of noise, which the witnesses described as sounding like the "squeak" of a huge mouse. Both young women were now crying hysterically. On the trip back to Point Pleasant, the huge thing cast a dark shadow over the rear window. The creature followed them all the way into town. Emitting its screeching sound like "a big mouse," at the Point Pleasant town limits, the creature turned away and was not seen again.

Still unnerved by their encounter, the two couples went directly to the Mason County Courthouse, where they excitedly sought out law enforcement authorities to make a report. The four witnesses proceeded to Deputy Sheriff Mallard Halstead's office, where they recounted their experience. Officers went to the scene at the TNT area, but they found nothing unusual. However, they experienced some scary moments. The two couples were there when a deputy saw "shadows circling" the old power plant. And Halstead admitted he saw a cloud of dust kick up from an adjacent coal yard that may have been the creature's doing. The sheriff's deputy took their testimony seriously when he saw how terrified the witnesses were. Mallette, Scarberry, and deputies returned Wednesday during the daylight and said they saw something fly up inside a boiler when a door was kicked open. No one stayed around long enough to see what it was, however.

The story about the Point Pleasant birdman was soon carried over the local news media, and "Mothman" became the hot topic of the Ohio Valley. When the first TNT sighting reached print, the four young people were the laughing stock of the town. But they had expected that. Steve Mallette told the local newspaper: "We understand people are laughing at us. But we wouldn't make up all this to make us look like fools." But that attitude would soon change, as old stories and new ones began to surface. Posses were even assembled at night to seek out the monster, though those armed groups would never manage to kill or capture the Mothman. People began to see the Mothman and talk openly about their encounters.

In what seems to have been a related incident about 90 miles away in Salem, West Virginia, Newell Partridge reported that, at about 10:30 PM that same evening, November 15, 1966, he had been watching television when suddenly his TV began flickering, then shut down. Bandit, Partridge's three-year old, pure-breed German Shepherd, began howling. Going outside with a flashlight, the Doddridge County farmer saw two large red eyes staring at him. Bandit took off towards the eyes, which then vanished. Partridge reported that he heard Bandit screech. He never saw his dog again.

Partridge's description of what he called the "red reflectors" matched the reports of the four young Mason County people who had had their TNT encounter about 90 minutes after Partridge's experience occurred. And in a detail that has often been overlooked in the chronicling of these two incidents, Partridge's report has a strange link with the Scarberrys and Mallettes account: the couples reported to the authorities that they had seen a dead dog on the roadside as they were being chased by the "thing." The four Point Pleasant residents noticed that when they returned to the TNT area with the sheriff's deputies, less an hour later, the dog's carcass was gone.

Point Pleasant's Nightmare

But that was only the beginning of the ordeal.

The very next night, Mothman put in another appearance. The witnesses were Mr. and Mrs. Raymond Wamsley and their friend, Mrs. Marcella Bennett, who had driven through the bunkers while on their way to visit a friend, Ralph Thomas, then superintendent of the Trojan-U.S. operations in Point Pleasant. Thomas lived in a bungalow among the TNT bunkers. After parking the car in a darkened area several feet from the residence, the witnesses approached and knocked on Thomas's door. When they were told their friend was not at home, they headed back to their vehicle. It was then that they saw a dark, shadowy figure lurking behind the automobile.

"It rose up slowly from the ground. A big, gray thing. Bigger than a man, with terrible, glowing, red eyes," said Bennett. (Along with Linda Scarberry, Bennett is one of the handful of witnesses featured in the David Grabias documentary on Mothman.)

When Bennett saw the creature, she became so horrified that she dropped her baby, whom she had been clasping tightly in her arms. The monster was a huge manlike figure with hideous glowing eyes, and the witnesses stood there in the dark almost paralyzed with fright as the figure slowly extended batlike wings from its back. Moments later, they sped back to Thomas's house and phoned the sheriff's department.

There were dozens of Mothman sightings during the next several weeks. One witness, Mrs. Roy Grose, who lived in the nearby town of Cheshire, saw the creature early one morning when her barking dog awakened her. Looking out the kitchen window, she saw a large multicolored object hovering over a treetop in a field across the road from her house. That same day a local teenager driving near Mrs. Grose's house encountered a huge "bird" which dived and followed his car. It chased him for about a mile.

The events of November 15, 1966 caused Kenneth Duncan to come forth with his November 12th sighting. He had seen something like a brown human being gliding through the trees near Clendenin, West Virginia, as he and others were digging a grave. On November 20, a couple reported that they had seen a large bird with a truckwide wingspan near Ferry Branch. It flew over their truck, landed in a tree, then flew up Ferry Branch Hollow. On the same day Howard Miller reported a bird "about four feet tall with red half-moons under his eyes." It landed on a school bus shelter in Dixie, Nicholas County. Also, Brenda Jones of Point Lick saw one beside a rock quarry at Campbell's Creek. It ran into the woods.

On the morning of November 25, Thomas Ury of Clarksburg, while eight miles north of Point Pleasant, saw a six-foot manlike creature with ten-foot wings. It hovered over his car and then flew toward the Ohio River. Tom Ury was a young shoe salesman at the time he saw the monster. He had no doubt heard of Mothman, but he really wasn't too interested in the creature as he drove down Route 62 at 7:15 that morning. He was merely on his way to work and minding his own business when he saw a towering figure standing by the road in an adjacent field.

"Suddenly it spread a pair of wings, and took off straight up, like a helicopter," he later told reporters. The figure then flew over his car and circled it like a bird. "It kept flying right over my car even though I was driving seventy-five," he added.

"I was so scared I just couldn't go to work that day. The thing had a wing span every bit of ten feet. It could be a bird, but I certainly never saw one like it. I was afraid it was going to come down right on top of me."

The next day on Cat Creek near Lowell, Ohio, the most extraordinary experience of all took place. For more than two hours several people watched four large birds that sat in bare trees and flew about the area. Two farmers, Marvin Shock and Ewing Tilton, and Shock's children watched them in daylight. The birds were four to five feet tall. Their wings spread out ten feet or more. Their breasts were charcoal gray; their backs were dark brown with light flecks. Their eyes could not be described. Shock thought there was a "reddish cast" to their heads and their bills were straight and 5 to 6 inches long.

Other brief encounters followed for almost a year, the record of which only appeared in news articles that Mark Hall and others have rediscovered. On November 27, 1966, near New Haven, West Virginia, Connie Jo Carpenter saw a creature fly toward her car. The next day, Richard West called the police to say a red-eyed six-foot tall manlike thing with a six-to-eight feet wingspan was on the roof next door. It flew straight into the air when it departed. On December 7, in Ohio near the Athens-Hocking county line on Route 33 a car nearly collided with a giant bird. The four women in the car all described a giant bird. On December 11, Kathryn Beaver reported that something big flew over her car near Wilson Straight in West Virginia.

Mothman was also seen in several towns neighboring Point Pleasant. One witness, an elderly businessman in Point Pleasant, even saw Mothman standing on his front lawn in full sight one night. He, too, noted that the figure was over six feet tall, gray, and was endowed with flaming eyes. As he watched, the birdman flew off like some gargoyle out of a Grade-B science fiction movie. Just about everybody who saw Mothman agreed on what it looked like, and they also agreed on their reactions to it. No one who saw it was indifferent to the creature, as somehow the thing struck terror into the hearts of all its viewers.

Point Pleasant in a Test Tube

One family that appeared to be a focus of activity and a reflection of the melodrama of Mothman was the McDaniels. On January 11, 1967, Mrs. Mabel McDaniel, Linda Scarberry's mother, had her only sighting of a large winged creature over Route 62, near Tiny's drive-in restaurant, at 5:00 PM

"I thought it was an airplane, then I realized it was flying much too low," she reported. "It was brown and had a wingspread of at least ten feet. I thought I could see two legs...like men's legs...hanging down from it. It circled over Tiny's and then flew off." The thing didn't seem to have a head or neck.

John Keel discussed the McDaniel family troubles in his book, *Strange Creatures from Time and Space*:

> The McDaniel family had been living in the twilight zone ever since their daughter and the others had first glimpsed "Mothman." Linda had repeatedly heard the sound "of a speeded-up phonograph record" around her own home after the incident, and peculiar manifestations indicating the presence of a poltergeist began. Finally she and Roger moved into the basement apartment in the McDaniel's home. The poltergeist followed them. Strange lights appeared in the house, objects moved by themselves, and the heavy odor of cigar smoke was frequently noted. No one in the family smokes. (The smell of cigar smoke is commonly reported in many poltergeist cases throughout the world.) One morning Linda woke up and distinctly saw the shadowy form of a large man in the room. The house was searched. All the doors were still locked. There was no sign of a prowler.

The McDaniels' experience was one of many during the thirteen intense months of the Mothman flap. Keel estimated that there were about a hundred sightings of Mothman, along with UFO sightings, poltergeist activity, Men-In-Black (MIBs) harassment, and other weird phenomena in the area. Other writers have recognized just how unusual this wave of activity really was, even outside of the actual reports of Mothman. For example, conspiracy author Jim Keith has written about this period as a time of "MIBs in a Test Tube" in his *Casebook on the Men in Black*. Weird MIB visitations, unreal near-kidnappings, strange human crimes, and grisly dog mutilations were widespread during the flap. The phenomena spilled over from the Mothman events and touched humans in ways they could not understand. Keith developed an elaborate theory that Point Pleasant was picked as a CIA experiment, a black ops (for an intelligence service's black operations) to see how Americans would react to a Cold War "flying saucer" disinformation invasion from the Soviets or others. The MIBs were disguised CIA or other intelligence agents.

(In one of those strange twists of fate that seem to follow those who investigate Mothman, Jim Keith at 50, died mysteriously, on September 7, 1999, during routine knee surgery after falling off the stage at the annual Burning Man pagan arts festival in Nevada. In a further bizarre twist, the publisher of most of Jim Keith's books, and of John Keel's 1991 reprint of *The Mothman Prophecies*, Ron Bonds of IllumiNet Press, died at the age of 48 on April 8, 2001, under strange circumstances while in the hospital being treated for food poisoning. It's understandable why John Keel talked about paranoia being merely a reasonable level of awareness when dealing with Mothman and MIBs.)

Strange events continued to occur in Point Pleasant in 1967. John Keel began receiving peculiar phone calls from people claiming to be in contact with aliens who made predictions of future events. Some of these are supposed to have been a warning that the Pope would be stabbed, that Robert Kennedy was in danger, and that the Silver Bridge, a suspension bridge (like a smaller version of the Golden Gate Bridge) between Kanauga, Ohio and Point Pleasant, West Virginia, would be destroyed.

Onward to the Silver Bridge

A correspondent for the Athens, Ohio, *Messenger,* Mary Hyre became a close friend of John A. Keel's. After feeding sightings and stories to him for months, they teamed up to interview witnesses and do on-site field work. On November 19, 1967, she told Keel: "I had a terrible nightmare. There were a lot of people drowning in the river and Christmas packages were floating everywhere in the water…it's like something awful is going to happen."

When Keel returned to Point Pleasant around Thanksgiving 1967, he had a flat tire in the rain. His trip was a string of miseries. And people in the area were having dreams and nightmares about a coming disaster. Virginia Thomas had them about people dying in the water of the nearby Ohio River.

And, indeed, at 5:04 PM, on December 15, 1967, the Silver Bridge collapsed during rush hour. "Everyone heard the low moaning of metal…and then the metal screamed," wrote Robert A. Goerman in a recent *Fate* article "Mothmania." Goerman explains why the bridge fell: "The final analysis conducted by the U.S. Department of Transportation ruled that the number 13 eyebar pin (on the upriver or north side of the bridge and west of the Ohio tower) had failed, causing the eyebar chain to drop below the roadway. The down-river eyebar was unable to support the weight of the entire structure, resulting in immediate, complete failure of the span."

Cars loaded with Christmas packages, shoppers, commuters, and kids fell into the Ohio River. A couple sightings of Mothman were said to have occurred near the bridge right before its collapse.

Keel was watching television in New York, preparing for a blackout he had expected when President Lyndon Johnson turned on the giant Christmas tree at the White House. Instead, a news bulletin interrupted the program telling of a bridge collapse in Gallopolis, Ohio. Keel knew there was no bridge at Gallopolis; the nearest bridge was down river, at Point Pleasant. Chills went up his spine. He tried for what seemed like hours to get through to Mary Hyre, to find out what was going on. When he reached her, she said, yes, she was safe, though she had been about to travel over the bridge herself when it happened. It was awful. So many dead. So horrible. And just like the nightmares.

Forty-six lives were lost, and forty-four bodies were recovered. Never before published in a book on Mothman, here are the names of those whose bodies were recovered:

> Albert A. Adler, Jr, Gallipolis, OH
> J. O. Bennnett, Walnut Cove, NC
> Leo Blackman, Richmond, VA
> Kristye Boggs, Vinton, OH
> Margaret Boggs, Vinton, OH

Hilda Byus, Point Pleasant, WV
Kimberly Byus, Point Pleasant, WV
Melvin Cantrell, Gallipolis Ferry, WV
Thomas A. Cantrell, Gallipolis, OH
Donna Jean Casey, Galliipolis, OH
Cecil Counts, Gallipolis Ferry, WV
Horace Cremeans, Route 1, Gallipolis, OH
Harold Cundiff, Winston-Salem, NC
Alonzo Luther Darst, Cheshire, OH
Alma Duff, Point Pleasant, WV
James Hawkins, Westerville, OH
Bobby L. Head, Gallipolis, OH
Forrest Raymond Higley, Bidwell, OH
Alva B. Lane, Route 1, Gallipolis, OH
Thomas "Bus" Howard Lee, Gallipolis, OH
G. H. Mabe, Jamestown, NC
Darlene Mayes, Kanauga, OH
Gerald McMannus, South Point, OH
James Richard Maxwell, Gallipolis, OH
James F. Meadows, Point Pleasant, WV
Timothy Meadows, Point Pleasant, WV
Frederick D. Miller, Gallipolis, OH
Ronnie G. Moore, Gallipolis, OH
Nora Isabelle Nibert, Gallipolis Ferry, WV
Darius E. Northup, Gallipolis Ferry, WV
James O. Pullen, Middleport, OH
Leo "Doc" Sanders, Point Pleasant, WV
Ronald Sims, Gallipolis, OH
Charles T. Smith, Bidwell, OH
Oma Mae Smith, Bidwell, OH
Maxine Sturgeon, Kanauga, OH
Denzil Taylor, Point Pleasant, WV
Glenna Mae Taylor, Point Pleasant, WV
Robert Eugene Towe, Cana, VA
Victor William Turner, Point Pleasant, WV
Marvin Wamsley, Point Pleasant, WV

Lillian Eleanor Wedge, Point Pleasant, WV
Paul D. Wedge, Point Pleasant, WV
James Alfred White, Point Pleasant, WV
The two whose bodies were never recovered are:

Kathy Byus, Point Pleasant, WV
Maxine Turner, Point Pleasant, WV

Some relatives of the major Mothman witnesses died in the collapse, and rumors indicated that some minor eyewitnesses of the winged weirdies were also killed. Whatever the truth of this shaky Mothman connection, many local people were touched by this tragedy. From my discussions with the residents of Point Pleasant, the bridge's destruction is forever linked to Mothman in the area and its impact has been great. People say they still see Mothman around the area but they are very reluctant to talk to officials about it.

When the David Grabias-produced 2002 documentary *Search for the Mothman* was in production, the crew interviewed Linda Scarberry for ten minutes but then had to stop the taping when on location at the TNT area. Linda's post-traumatic feeling rushed forth, and she became too overwhelmed to go any further. Her ex-husband, Roger, lately of Charleston, West Virginia, refused to be interviewed, as did the Mallettes. Linda Scarberry and other eyewitnesses remain shaken by the events of 1966-1967 and have a difficult time reliving them.

So what eventually happened to Mothman? Like so many monsters, Mothman just seemed to appear less frequently and then disappeared from West Virginia completely several months after it had first been seen. It never attacked anyone, never tried to communicate, nor took much notice of the people it terrified. It just liked to chase cars every once in a while as though the automobile was as intriguing to it as it was to those who saw it. It seemed to be something alien to our world, though momentarily trapped in it. It almost seems as though Mothman was someone's nightmare that had been objectified into physical existence.

We don't know who or what Mothman was, or is. But it is not unique in the lore of monsters. In looking over all the reports in this book, it certainly looks as though the birdmen seen in Houston, Cornwall, Vietnam, and West Virginia were all blood relatives. They were all dark-skinned, all winged, and most were slightly larger than normal human beings. Many of them appeared to glow, or had glowing eyes, and many had the strange habit of taking off straight into the air. So it appears that our planet might have been momentarily inhabited by a race of otherworldly creatures. Was Mothman a monster, cryptid, alien, or a ghost that haunted Point Pleasant? Only when a Mothman is captured will we know for sure, although it is really doubtful whether that will ever happen.

The Sound of a Monster

Often encountered, but never caught. This appears to be the legacy of Mothman, which has haunted us all long after its last sighting.

In April 1976, after Jerome Clark had returned home from his investigatory jaunt through the Rio Grande Valley, talking to eyewitnesses about the weird batman reports down there, he was interviewed by telephone by Vic Wheatman, who co-hosted with me a Fortean radio show on Boston's WBUR-FM. The interview, taped for later broadcast (it eventually aired May 24), went without incident. It was only when Wheatman and I had the technical staff play the tape back that we realized something extremely odd had occurred.

Midway through the conversation, I had asked Clark if he saw any similarity between the Texas Big Bird reports and the "Mothman" reports ten years earlier. "Very definite similarity," Clark replied. "Now, John Keel, of course, is the man who did the research on Mothman. Keel claimed that there is a connection between these sightings and UFOs. If there's any such connection with the Big Bird, I was unable to prove it....All I know is that this thing doesn't have any business existing in the Rio Grande Valley or anywhere. This is really something out of the ordinary. I have no idea where it is coming from."

As he spoke these lines, Clark heard nothing out of the ordinary on his end. Neither did Wheatman and I on ours. Yet on the tape, immediately after the word "sightings" in the third sentence, there is a loud, unmistakable and very startling EEPPP! sound—precisely the sound Mothman is supposed to have made. ("It squeaked like a big mouse," one of the original Mothman witnesses had commented in 1966.)

When radio station personnel heard the sound, they could offer no explanation, unless it originated with Clark, which it didn't. It remains a spooky episode in our lives, and makes us wonder about the mechanisms of this phenomena.

Theories

For some critics, there is nothing in the original accounts of the "Mothman" sightings that cannot be explained by misidentifications of a few sandhill cranes or turkey vultures.

After the initial November 1966 sightings of Mothman in the TNT area near Point Pleasant, Robert Smith of the biology department at West Virginia University was reported to have said he thought it was a sighting of a rare sandhill crane. Zoologists at Ohio University, however, pointed out that the crane would be a rare sight indeed in Ohio and West Virginia, since it lived on the plains of Canada. Shown pictures of the sandhill crane, witness Roger Scarberry scoffed at the suggestion. Mary Mallette, who also saw it, said: "I just wish Dr. Smith could see the thing."

The gathering of all reports under the umbrella term, "Mothman," was unfortunate. John Keel's interviews and later writings tend to lump all of the large, man-sized, gray-bodied, red-glowing eyed creature reports together. While any of us, with hindsight, can now clearly see that *some* of these reports were entirely mundane bird sightings, Keel was in the middle of a vortex. Separating the wheat from the chaff must have been difficult as he was bombarded with new reports and his own personal saga of troubles in Point Pleasant. But real birds were undoubtedly part of the mix.

In the midst of the flap, a snowy owl and a turkey vulture were "caught." A detailed multiple witness sighting in Lowell, Ohio, near Cat's Creek (70 miles north of Point Pleasant), on November 26, 1966, had four people seeing a flock of four large birds in some trees for two hours. Eyewitness Ewing Tilton said they appeared to be 4-5 feet tall with a 10 foot wingspan. "They had dark brown backs with some light flecks. Their breasts were gray and they had five- to six-inch bills, straight, not curved like those of hawks or vultures," said Tilton. Another witness, Marvin Shock, reported the heads had a "reddish cast." This sighting may have been a view of common birds, needless to say, perhaps sandhill cranes.

Giant Owls

But clearly, other things were going on

Cryptozoologist Mark A. Hall, the author of a thought-provoking article called "Bighoot—The Giant Owl" in *Wonders* Vol. 5, No. 3., September 1998, theorizes that Mothman may be a giant species of undiscovered owl. Hall defines "Bighoot" [big + hoot, the traditional owl sound] as: "A bird of prey in the order Strigiformes. In size larger than all other owls. Never scientifically described. Observed in the wild in the eastern U.S.A. in the states of Ohio and West Virginia. Folklore of similar birds is found elsewhere in the world."

For cryptozoologists who tended to look for only eastern cougar and Bigfoot reports, especially in Ohio and West Virginia, a few reports of Bighoot may have been filed in their "strange things in the woods" file. Hall cites a Bighoot report from Rocky Fork Lake in southern Ohio for August 1982, that turned up in the hominological newsletter *Bigfoot Coop*, published by a California anthropology professor, Connie Cameron.

Hall's treatment is the first clearly zoological and cryptozoological re-examination of the Mothman reports—separating the tangibles from the paranormal theories of John Keel. Hall lists evidence to link the Mothman sightings to a large unknown owl in the area.

Hall notes that these birds have been around Point Pleasant for a very long time, as their presence is noted in many Indian legends. The American Indians called them "Flying Heads" or "Big Head," quoting Iroquois, the Tuscarora, and the Wyandot Indians as saying, "They were huge, bodiless heads covered in long hair from which protruded sharp nailed claws. With open mouths and fiery eyes the Big Heads flew about in storms, the wind keeping them up by their masses of hair."

Researcher Hall uncovered this entry by William Connelly in this description among the Wyandots from Ohio: "The Flying Heads plagued the Wyandots. They were more dangerous and troublesome during rainy, foggy, or misty weather. They could enter a cloud of fog, or mist, or rime [ice], and in it approach a Wyandot village unseen. They were cruel and wicked hooh-kehs and cannibals. They caused sickness; they were vampires, and lay in wait for people, whom they caught and devoured. They carried away children; they blighted the tobacco and other crops; they stole and devoured the game after the hunter had killed it."

One surprising tidbit that Hall discovered was a report of a large bird from the early 1900s at Point Pleasant, West Virginia. It certainly sounds like a precursor to the Mothman accounts of years later—in exactly the right area. In a book called *Haunted Valley and More Folk Tales* by James Gay Jones, an emeritus professor of history at Glenville State College, Hall found this gem:

> In the early 1900's at Pt. Pleasant, a large bird with the head of a man and wingspan of at least 12 feet was seen. It appeared just prior to or immediately after the occurrence of a tragic event... It was also seen by rural farm families in Mason, Jackson, Roane, Clay and Kanawha counties. By World War I, birdman was observed flying over Looneyville, up Johnson Creek, down Gabe in Roane County thence down Elk Valley into the Kanawha. Its monstrous size and dark reddish feathers which glistened in the sunlight cast fear in all who saw it. Parents kept children indoors after sightings. After World War II people said they were chased by a huge bird while traveling on the highways of Mason, Jackson, and Wood counties near the Ohio River.

In the post- World War II era, Hall notes, people reported being chased by mysterious birds on the roads where Mothman would later be seen. "These birds, in common with the enormous Thunderbirds," he writes, "seem at times to take advantage of the artificial air currents created by automobiles. The effect on the humans in the vehicles is startling, but the birds are looking for a natural advantage. Soaring flight is important to large birds....It is their automobiles that have created this situation."

Mark Hall senses that Mothman/Bighoot may have developed a protective mimicry that "has been utilized by the giant owls to disguise themselves as upright trees and logs lying on the ground....An example of this mimicry in action comes in a report from a woman in Ohio who observed something she could not understand. She saw this thing at Rocky Fork Lake in southern Ohio around August of 1982. About a year later she saw a similar sight at the same lake." The witness said that "...while fishing in Rocky Fork Lake in Ohio we drifted into a pristine cove on the SW side and noted with utter disbelief an old tall topless tree truck approx 9-10 feet high, 112 inches around, move about 4 ft. sideline. (This was on shore about 20 ft. inland among like-looking trees, with underbrush.) Again it moved, only this time there was a partial twisting or rotation from the top 18-24 inches. It slowly maneuvered backward (keeping erect like a tree) into the woods with NO NOISES from it or underbrush as graceful as a bird thru a tree. It stopped in the mid of a sunlight clearing..." She then writes that "wings unfolded with a span greater than most small airplanes." After a while she reports it returned to its "tree appearance." She saw the "semblance of two eyes" and thought it was watching them. The sun went down and the sight was lost to view. Then: "One year later, same lake and a half mile or so from that first cove this figure appeared near shoreline again. (It seemed taller or leaner.) This time [I] got a look at its legs and feet—yellowish grainy like chicken legs...they were so thin and short for its height. Three long slender toes with a hooked toe or nail on lower leg."

For Hall, Bighoot, the North American giant owl, is the answer. Keeping an open mind, I see it as one option among many.

Why Mothman Belongs in Cryptozoology

Paleontologist and sometime cryptozoology author Darren Naish wrote an article in 2001 entitled "How to Approach a Winged Humanoid, " which appeared on the *Fortean Times* website. It's full of data about a few Gambian (Atlantic West African) cryptids or creatures or fantastic beasts, depending upon your point of view. Of course, your point of view is what his contribution is really all about. Some of these creatures, you see, appear to be winged humanoids, and we humans are very uncomfortable with the thought of winged humanoids. It seems zoologists are even more rattled by them. But my point is that cryptozoology does not just belong to zoologists.

The Gambian critters are a strange lot. For example, you have the *Kikiyaon* and the *Guiafairo*, which Naish writes are "both sharp-clawed flying monsters that appear to combine human and avian traits."

Then there's the *Sasabonsam*, which Naish observes is "traditionally a vampire or ogre-like monster from Ashanti myth, is sort of similar, though it was regarded by Heuvelmans as another name for the *kongamato* [an African winged cryptid, the name translates as "overwhelmer of watercraft," which some say looks like a giant bat or pterosaur]. Remarkably, a 1939 article published in *The West African Review* recounts the capture, killing and examination of a *sasabonsam* specimen. According to the account, the creature had a man-sized body with bat-like wing membranes attached to elongate clawed arms. The wingspan was something like 20 ft. Some of the features described are just bizarre—its hands were reported to be retractable and it apparently had a human-like nose and two short horns on its head. Other features are highly intriguing. For example, it had a prominent ridge down the middle of its chest (a sternal keel?). It had sharp teeth, stiff hair on its head and elongate, slim hindlegs. Needless to say this doesn't correspond to anything we know of."

In any case, Darren Naish uses the Gambian critters to launch into a discussion of what he calls, I must humbly note, "Loren's Paradigm." Naish views as "unlikely" the proposal by some, like me, who regard such creatures as "cryptids *sensu stricto*." "I've dubbed this 'Loren's paradigm', after cryptozoologist Loren Coleman," writes Naish, "though strictly speaking it's not Loren's and it's not a paradigm…Mark Hall, for example, apparently a strict applicator of Loren's paradigm, has argued that some of the feathery 'winged humanoids' may actually be gigantic owls, a notion I find pretty ludicrous."

Then he continues: "At the risk of sounding tedious, cryptozoology is a part of zoology, and the more trained academic zoologists we have contributing to cryptozoological problems, the better. One problem is that some researchers operating on the fringes of cryptozoology have no interest in subjecting their ideas to scientific scrutiny."

Darren Naish calls my approach "Loren's Paradigm" based mainly on thoughts I have written calling for a broad-based analysis of folklore and legends within the ranks of cryptozoology. In an email of March 22, 1999, Naish writes: "I can't help but think that by ostensibly including all manner of bizarre unknowns (including mythical flying and swimming humanoid creatures) within cryptozoology, we are truly creating an amorphous and undefinable field of study that clearly does not nest comfortably within the zoological framework: the framework that Heuvelmans tried to adhere to. Indeed, if we are to follow the definition that Loren suggests, are zoologists supposed to be coming up with a proposed biological and historical model to account for the identity and evolution of owlman, or mothman—much as ancient scholars did to account for sightings of angels? It is surely untenable that such things are real animals."

Of course, I wasn't speaking of angels, but of cryptids. Anyone reading Bernard Heuvelmans' works in the 1950s through the 1980s, clearly knows he was interested in a multidisclipinary approach to cryptozoology, a wide-ranging review of many forms of material which would inform a position of considerable knowledge regarding the possible zoological existence of new animals. Heuvelmans thought people should be well-read in myth, legend, and folklore, as well as botany, linguistics, and anthropology. That too much information is in some way inconvenient never crossed Heuvelmans' mind.

Naish has implied in his writings that too many creatures is an unfortunate situation, noting that more and more Mothman-like reports will cause a dilution of resources. However, the universe of cryptids was just as filled back in Heuvelmans' days as it is today. It seems like we should know more by now. Perhaps one reason that it appears that no new headway is being made in cryptozoology is that by the time something is scientifically verified, of course, it is of little interest to cryptozoologists. Heuvelmans wrote about reports of lemurs in his classic *On the Track of Unknown Animals*, and they have since been discovered. But people don't ponder this for very long. A whole new group of coelacanths have been found off Indonesia, but who talked about them in depth for any length of time? Cryptozoology, by its very nature, is fickle. Discover something and move on to the next mystery. Oh sure, we all talk about the okapi, the mountain gorilla, or the 1938 coelacanth, but how many "psychological autopsies" do we perform on what happened regarding John McKinnon's discoveries of the *saola* of Vietnam?

I think we are missing the boat, and we don't even know it passed by sometimes. This is not the time to "limit" and "screen out" what we examine and listen for in natives' and locals' eyewitness descriptions and physical evidence. Now is the time to expand our awareness of the reality that nature's mysteries are much more vast than any human can even attempt to realize. Our vision is limited by our humanness, not expanded by it. While I have a sense that "Loren's paradigm" is going places I never had in mind, I wholeheartedly embrace the notion that, as part of cryptozoology, we must be open to cryptids that native peoples make fantastic. Heuvelmans was clear about this, and I am, too.

Mothman is a case in point. I do not recall that I ever said anything much more than some of what was being termed "Mothman" may in fact be based on overblown and embellished accounts of giant owls (as per Mark A. Hall's discussion of finding reports from 100 years ago of giant owl-like avian creatures from the same West Virginia area as the Mothman sightings)—or even Bigfoot-like cryptids. To neglect the fire behind some reports of Mothman or winged weirdies is to ignore that Yeti, Kraken, and Sasquatch accounts have folkloric elements that are studied by cryptozoologists.

If a large animal with a ten-foot wingspan that has scared teenagers and Appalachian witnesses and chased their cars had been called something other than "Mothman," would we even be having this discussion? Does something issue from the media-driven importance of these creatures that disturb scientists? Why is it so easy to note that the Kongamato is part of cryptozoology, and yet have questions about Mothman?

Just because some of the reports that happen to be cryptid in nature and thus grist for the cryptozoological mill are labeled by media folk, tellers of tall tales, and locals as "Mothman" does not mean we should exclude all of these reports because of their "gathering moniker." If I feel some of what people call Mothman are instead misidentified unidentified birds, how do we know that part of what is being seen is a cryptid or not?

Remember, until an unknown or hidden animal is scientifically identified, it is a cryptid. Why should folklore about the Meh-teh of the Sherpas of the Himalayas be included in cryptozoological studies, and folklore of the Mothmen of the local people of Appalachia be excluded? In "Loren's Paradigm," they both belong in cryptozoology, and there seems enough evidence that *part* of the solutions in both cases could lie with real animals, either mundane, misidentified, or entirely new. Mothman is a cryptid, and belongs in cryptozoology.

Hades of Zoological Literature

The zoological classification of animals is the function of another branch of zoology, not cryptozoology. Cryptozoologists are the detectives who produce the evidence that new animals may exist. Bernard Heuvelmans was very specific in why he created the investigative pursuit that would later be called "Cryptozoology." Heuvelmans, in his *On the Track of Unknown Animals* (pp. xxiii-xxiv), wrote:

> In the 1950s, I was an angry young zoologist, indignant at the ostracism imposed by official science—we would say today the scientific Establishment—on those animals known only through the reports of isolated travelers, or through often fantastic native legends, or from simple but mysterious footprints, or the recital of sometimes bloody depredations, or through traditional images, or even a few ambiguous photos. Instances of this sort were, in fact, quite numerous. These were attested to by files, often quite thick, which in general gathered dust at the bottom of drawers or, at the most, were considered as "amusing curiosities." It would have been much better to term them "the secret archives of zoology," or even, since they were in some way shameful in the eyes of correct thinkers, "the Hades of zoological literature." It had in fact been decreed on high and, moreover, in a totally arbitrary fashion, that only those species for which there existed a representative specimen, duly registered in

some institution, or at the least an identifiable fragment of a specimen, could be admitted into zoological catalogues. Lacking this, they were banned from the Animal Kingdom, and zoologists were morally constrained to speak of them only with an exasperated shrug of the shoulder or a mocking smile.

To propose devoting a profound study to sea-serpents, the Abominable Snowman, the Loch Ness monster, or to all such-like, amounted to straightforward provocation. Furthermore, no scientific publication would have accepted it for printing unless, of course, it ended with the conclusion that the being in question was the result of popular imagination, founded on some misapprehension, or the product of a hoax. As for myself, however, in spite of my status as professional zoologist and my university degrees, I dreamed of delivering all of those condemned beasts from the ghetto in which they had so unjustly been confined, and to bring them to be received into the fold of zoology.

If we examine what fantastic tales existed before the formal establishing of a species, we will find many stories as bizarre as Mothman sounds to many ears today. Folklore and native traditions which speak of creatures seemingly "too bizarre" to some researchers should not be a valid excuse for ignoring them and refusing to decipher their zoological status, if any. A monster rumor from Africa, recorded as long ago as 1625 by the English explorer Andrew Battel, told of a giant that had a hollow-eyed face who went around "upon his legs" which killed many "Negroes" and beat to death elephants. This creature was never taken alive, and was so strong that ten men could not hold it. Of course, today we know that this animal, the Pongo, is the gorilla.

Heuvelmans wrote in *On the Track of Unknown Animals*, (page 58) that "as early as 1860 the natives of Rumanika in Ruanda (adjacent to Kivu) had told...of a monster which hugged women so savagely that they died. The negroes in the east of the Belgian Congo had always been full of tales about what was called *Ngagi* in Kiniaruanda and *Ngila* in Kiswaheli and Kingwana. But even though the whites had known the Gabon gorilla for some 40 years, they refused to believe these 'absurd legends' until Beringe killed the first specimen [of the mountain gorilla]."

The "largest sea-monster in the world," the many-armed Kraken, was considered absurd fiction until indisputable physical evidence of the existence of the giant squid put the tales in context. The "giant black pig," the Nigbwe, turned out to be the pygmy hippopotamus. There are many more such examples but I think the point is made.

Cryptozoology must put the same standards of insights and open-mindedness to the accounts of the Chupacabras and Mothman that have been placed on the Nigbwe, Ngagi, and Ngila. Notes Heuvelmans in *On the Track of Unknown Animals* (p. 82): "There is not a single example of a large animal which has remained quite unnoticed by the people who live nearest its habitat. The local descriptions of the beast are often only roughly accurate and exaggerated in some respects. Sometimes the animal is said to have supernatural powers." As Heuvelmans noted in his day, critics often placed little trust in the legends and stories of so-called "primitives." Heuvelmans called for a revision of that view, noting that the "most fantastic and incredible traditions" of "primitive tribes" had an "origin in fact."

This cultural elitism that Heuvelmans spoke of also appears to be at play with regard to the view of AngloAmerican critics of the rural Appalachian reports of Mothman and the Hispanic accounts of the Chupacabras, which we will examining later in this book. Excluding reports because the data you have collected or read means it does not fit your notion of what a "real animal" is, should not apply to serious cryptozoological inquiry. We cannot pre-screen witnesses and only accept what we sense is zoological reality. Had this been done in the past, many clues and links—and ultimately animals—would have been overlooked. Many cryptid accounts, modern and old, are indeed "fantastic," but that does not mean they should not be collected and analyzed.

Furthermore, the first-hand eyewitness testimony on Mothman and Chupacabras appears to pass the litmus tests that some would erect that might keep out secondhand tales of the Kraken. You cannot have it both ways; you cannot allow only the tales you like because they match former cryptids that are now known animals while setting unrealistic guidelines for accounts you dislike in the modern era. Well, of course, you can, but I mean to say, this is not good science. A cryptid is a supposed animal that has not been identified, to date. Nothing more, nothing less.

Looking at the reports of Mothman, in its essence, you have firsthand sightings of a giant gray birdlike animal with red eyes. Some witnesses reported ten foot wingspans, some said the eyes glowed. These fantastic elements should not be held against examining these reports. John Keel wrote that witnesses "felt" their cars were traveling at a high speed when being chased by these avian cryptids. Keel's writings, the Mothman label, and the witnesses' psychology are merely the canvas. We must look at what lies beneath all these accounts.

Examine all parts of the Mothman file, not just the fantastic ones. Large birds were seen in the area at least back as far as the early 1900s. Reread the statements of Captain Paul Yoder and Benjamin Enochs who saw a large animal on November 18, 1966, in the TNT area, that "was definitely a bird with big red eyes...huge...never seen anything like it." Think about the November 26, 1966, report by four witnesses who saw four gigantic birds, that seemed to have ten foot wingspans and six-inch long bills. There is more to the Mothman than meets the eye.

Perhaps, as some believe, Mothman was a combination of mass hysteria, sandhill cranes, unknown giant owls related to the huge extinct owl, *Ornimegalonyx oteroi* from Pleistocene Cuba, or more. But if we exclude Mothman from cryptozoological discussions, we allow the valid zoological evidence which may lie within these reports of unknown animals to be taken over by paranormalists and demonologists. Or to be lost to urban legend collectors who could care less if a real animal exists in the mix. Do cryptozoologists want to allow this to happen? I don't.

For those few cryptozoologists who wish to ostracize and assign Mothman to the Hades of zoological literature, I propose they reexamine the origins of cryptozoology and the place folklore serves in support of our studies. As correspondent Jan Williams has written me about the paradigm discussion: "The bondegezou (*Dendrolagus mbaiso*) of Irian Jaya is surely a good example of the dangers of ignoring folklore reports, whether ancient or modern. What self-respecting investigator would take notice of a 'man of the forest' with a white star on its fore-head, which responded to people by throwing out its arms in greeting and whistling? Especially when the Moni tribespeople referred to it as the sacred spirit of their ancestors? Luckily Tim Flannery's expedition found this primitive tree kangaroo."

I speak for open-mindedness, for looking at the evidence of possible zoological components within reports, sightings, encounters, and tales of mundane-to-seemingly-fantastic beasts, whether reported in the hills of Irian Jaya or those of Appalachia. But it is a misrepresentation to say that my whole focus is only promoting or saying that Mothman *is* definitely a giant owl. What I am attempting to convey is that Mothman is a cryptid which may turn out to be a variety of things—I advocate taking a combined Fortean and cryptozoology view of this mystery. It is a classic cryptozoological exercise to examine the facts, sightings, and local traditions regarding animate flying cryptids located in West Virginia. It is Fortean to remain open minded to a variety of answers. Remember, labeling something a *cryptid* does not mean that it someday will become part of zoology as a new species of animal. All it means is that there is a body of evidence existing for us to analyze what such and such a cryptid might be. To make a cryptid into a bonafide animal before there is evidence is to have skipped some investigative steps. We should not be as guilty as the zoologists who we have criticized for years for ignoring the native accounts of the pygmy hippos, the okapis, and the mountain gorillas because the very existence of these cryptids went beyond Cuvier's dictum. Some cryptids will turn out to be animals (new, rediscovered, out-of-place, and/or misidentified ones), while others will turn out to be fog, hysteria, logs, rocks, and the like. We do not know unless we look, and if some schools of thought are saying we should not even do any cryptozoological research because something is locally called Mothman, well, I think that defeats the whole underlying mission of cryptozoology.

Now the Movie
In 2000, Richard Gere took on the leading role in *The Mothman Prophecies,* a psychological thriller based on the nonfiction book of the same name by John Keel. The movie began production in January, 2001,

and premiered in early 2002. Gere plays a newspaper reporter investigating a series of UFO reports and other strange events in a small town. The film, set contemporarily, tells the story of a recently widowed reporter, played by Gere, who is drawn to the West Virginia town of Point Pleasant to investigate strange events, including psychic visions, UFOs and the appearance of a flying creature known as Mothman. "Based on a true story," as they say. Lakeshore Entertainment financed the project.

The film released domestically by Sony/Screen Gems, has Mark Pellington as its director who previously steered the creepy conspiracy film *Arlington Road* to the screen. Film crews used a small town in western Pennsylvania as the location for the shooting of the film. Local churches, bridges, and restaurants, as well as the county courthouse, of Kittanning took the place of Point Pleasant. The Kittanning Bridge stood in for the Silver Bridge. The reporter, of course, is loosely based on John Keel, and then there's the Chicago-based character, the enigmatic Dr. Leek. The moniker is "Keel" spelled backwards, needless to say, and it is a nod to the name game. See if you can pick out other in-jokes that director Mark Pellington has sprinkled throughout the motion picture, like the numbers game (e.g., related to the mysterious number 23) linked to the supposed time that the Will Patton character thinks "John Klein" is knocking at his home's door.

The movie is the story of John Klein, whose wife dies suddenly of a brain tumor, and exactly two years later he finds himself in the town of Point Pleasant, West Virginia—even though he'd been heading for a destination hundreds of miles in another direction. Strange things are happening in Point Pleasant—a farmer thinks Klein has come to his door three nights in a row, even though Klein just arrived in town, for instance. This same man later describes his encounter with a sort-of human named Indrid Cold who has given him information on an earth-quake—this premonition comes true. Eventually, the weight of the weirdness gets to Klein, who fears he won't be able to stop a great tragedy that has been foreseen from occurring. He returns to Georgetown, but is beckoned back to Point Pleasant by his new love, the local sheriff. A twist at the end is intriguing, and I am not going to give it away here. The twist does, however, provide for a visual climax.

I hope the excitement generated by the new movie and the David Grabias directed and produced documentary helps educate a new generation to the wonder and mystery of Mothman.

The News Even Now Comes In

While a fictional Mothman's red eyes glare from the screen, the real Mothman may still be around, in different but familiar guises. On November 5, 2001, *The Bristol Press* of Connecticut carried a small news item telling of how a Nicholas Drive man called police on Sunday, November 4th, to report that he saw an unidentified flying object at about 1:00 AM that morning, hovering near the Beals Community Center. The Bristol resident said that while he was walking his dog, he looked up to see something like a bird with flapping wings—but it was the size of an ultra light airplane and produced "a whirring, almost mechanical sound."

And so it goes.

CHAPTER 4

Thunderbirds

During 2001, I interviewed a thirty-five year old man who had an extraordinary experience when he was eleven. He grew up playing in the Alabama woods and was very active outdoors. As a "country boy," he was well acquainted with the wildlife, the mammals and birds of his area, so when he had his encounter with a large condorlike bird with a five to six foot tall body and wingspan three times as large, he knew he had seen something out of the ordinary. Today, he still wishes his parents would have known whom to contact instead of dismissing it as a large ordinary condor. But then, people have been dismissing these sightings for more than two hundred years.

Michael Hallmark is one of those ordinary people who have encountered an unusual creature, which no zoological textbook can help them understand. His sighting of an extremely large bird took place in Oneonta, Alabama, a town about 25 miles northeast of Birmingham, near the family home where he grew up and which is still occupied by his father.

The youth was first alerted by a shadow larger than he had ever seen which blocked out the sun for a second or two. When he looked directly above, he saw a huge bird with a wingspan of about 15 feet, tip to tip, sailing overhead. The bird was "eagle like," he thought, with all parts of its anatomy being much bigger. Its body was roughly bigger than his own body; its color was dark brown, almost black.

The wings were about 4 feet wide. It was the most incredible thing he had ever seen, he told me. He watched it for about 10 seconds and panicked, running back into his home. Down through the years, Michael Hallmark has not talked about his sighting, but with older age, he now knows that just because people dismissed the sighting by saying it was probably an escaped condor, doesn't mean that it is so. What a condor would be doing in Alabama in the 1970s is something no one can answer. But what Hallback and other witnesses have learned is that there is an old body of sightings, those known as Thunderbirds, which serves as a starting point for a discussion of such encounters.

Indian America's Thunderbirds

Native Americans were excellent chroniclers of the natural world. They often spoke, in great depth and across tribal groups, about giant flying creatures they called "thunderbirds." The word has now become part of America's modern culture, denoting everything from a very cheap wine to a classic automobile. Most people associate the maker of thunder as a part of Old West legends. The relationship between thunderbirds and thunderstorms may be obvious, but to restate it, the general belief is that myth-making Indians felt the giant birds of the plains "made" the lightning, the thunder, and the storms. The closely observing natives, however, seem more often than not to have been discussing the use of these weather patterns and storm systems as a means by which these thunderbirds would travel and migrate. Many Cheyennes, Arapahos, Comanches, and other Native Americans claim to have actually seen one or more thunderbirds during their lives. To the Native Americans, the birds were more than mythological creatures; the thunderbirds were real animals.

And reports of real thunderbirds continue today. Modern sightings of Thunderbirds, following the pattern from the ancient traditions of the Indians, are found from Appalachia and the Black Forest of Pennsylvania to the plains of Illinois and the Ozarks of Arkansas.

Illinois' Postwar Thunderbirds

Although the sightings of these massive feathered wonders have occurred in both the West and the East, I find it much more illustrative to concentrate on one hotspot of accounts. A particularly interesting cluster of thunderbird sightings have issued from the state of Illinois.

When I was in my twenties, I spent many weeks digging through newspaper archives at libraries and universities throughout Illinois and Missouri to uncover the exacting details of the whole series of sightings that took place in 1948.

The first sighting for which the newspapers took notice occurred on 9 April 1948 on a farm outside Caledonia, Illinois, where Mr. and Mrs. Robert Price saw what they called "a monster bird...bigger than an airplane." It had a long neck, huge powerful wings, and in Robert Price's words, "what I suppose were its feet trailing behind it." It flew out of sight toward the northeast.

Shortly afterwards, a Freeport, Illinois truck driver came forth with corroborating testimony admitting that he had seen the huge creature from a different location on the same day. "I saw the bird," Veryl Babb said. "But at first I didn't say anything because I thought people would laugh at me. When I read that Price had seen it, I decided to report all about it."

A former army colonel then related that nearly a week earlier, on April 4th, a gigantic bird had passed four thousand feet above him while he stood talking with Colonel Ralph Jackson, head of Western Military Academy, and a farmer near Alton, Illinois. He did not point it out to his companions. "It looked too incredible. I thought there was something wrong with my eyesight," said Walter F. Siegmund, wartime commander of the Kearns, Utah Army Air Force base. "But it was definitely a bird and not a glider or jet plane. It appeared to be flying northeast. Two Army planes had just flown over in the same direction, and I thought it was a pursuit craft following them. But from the movements of the object and its size, I figured it could only be a bird of some tremendous size."

Old Cases Revived

Because of the media interest in these strange stories of big birds seen in the sky, an even older story turned up. It was a twelve-year-old boy named James Trares, who first sighted the mysterious bird, but he had only discussed the details of his sighting with his parents. Now, the Trares went to the papers with their story. Three months before, in January 1948, James was playing outside his parents' Mohier Drive home in Glendale, Illinois, just before sunset. Suddenly, he saw something that sent him scurrying inside to his mother, Mrs. Trares. "There's a bird outside as big as a B-29!" he exclaimed breathlessly. He said he knew it was not a plane because he saw its wings flapping. The creature was gray-green in color and flying toward the sun. The Trares story, and an earlier one from Ramone, Ontario, may indicate the big bird was around long before the April reports of 1948.

In the Midst of a Flap

Anyway, the reports did continue. On April 10, 1948, the day after the Price and Babb sightings in Caledonia, the bird appeared over Overland, Illinois and was sighted by Mr. and Mrs. Clyde C. Smith and Les Bacon. They said they thought it was a pursuit plane until it began to flap its wings furiously. The big bird appeared to be dark gray in color from where they viewed it in the Smiths' backyard just before noon. As it happened, it was Clyde Smith's second sighting of the day. "I first saw it when I was out in the yard that morning," he said later, "and I thought it was a type of plane I had never seen before. It was circling and banking in a way I had never seen a plane perform, and I kept waiting for it to fall."

A week later, on the eighteenth, Chet Burke of Richmond Heights, Illinois, reported that a strange bird passed over his house. But this one was much smaller than a plane and resembled an albatross, a seabird with a seven-foot wingspan that does not ever come as far inland as western Illinois. In fact, officially, no albatross has ever been seen west of Maine.

On April 24th a more impressive report was made at Alton, Illinois where E.M. Coleman and his fifteen-year-old son James gazed at an astonishing sight. "It was an enormous, incredible thing with a body that looked like a naval torpedo," E.M. Coleman said. "It was flying at about five hundred feet and cast a shadow the same size as that of a Piper Cub at the same height."

Patrolmen Clarence Johnson and Francis Hennelly of the St. Louis Police Department got a look at the bird as it flew silhouetted against the moon that same night. "The thing was as big as a small airplane," Hennelly said. "Its wings were flapping, and it was headed southwest, flying at an altitude of several hundred feet. I thought it was a large eagle, but I've never seen one that big before."

A Doctor's Description

Two days later, on April 26, 1948, a St. Louis-based Doctor of Chiropractic, Kristine Dolezal, had just finished breakfasting in her second floor apartment. About 8:40 AM, she got up from the table and started across the kitchen. Suddenly the sounds of a nearby airplane flying low over the house broke the silence. "It sounded like something was wrong with the motor, " Dolezal commented later. "It sort of roared and sputtered." She stepped out onto the porch to see what was wrong but was hardly prepared for what greeted her. "I looked at the plane, then I glanced over the other way, " she reported. "I saw this bird just come from nowhere it seemed like. I thought, What is it? Is it a big bird, or what?" As the creature came nearer it seemed inexplicably to grow larger. Dolezal at first thought her eyes were playing tricks on her, but then she realized it had spread its wings, which previously had been folded back. In the meantime, the plane changed course, and for a moment it looked like the bird and plane were about to collide. But the bird flapped its wings lazily three times, and both bird and plane vanished into the clouds.

In the May 2, 1948 issue of *Everyday Magazine* which appeared in the *St. Louis Post Dispatch*, writer Dickson Terry noted, "Like others who have seen the thing, Dr. Dolezal describes it as grayish-black in color. Her description of the deliberate beating of the huge wings also jibes with other descriptions. However, where others describe it as having no tail to speak of, the thing she saw had, she says, quite an exceptional tail. It was like a rectangular box, which had been sawed or divided down the center. When its (wings) were spread, she said, she could see ridges across them, like the ribs which show beneath the covering on the wings of a plane."

The following day, instructors at the Mississippi School of Aeronautics at Lambert-St. Louis Field sighted an "awfully big bird" at an altitude of about twelve hundred feet. A little more than 24 hours later salesman Harry Bradford saw the bird as he was turning off the Red Feather Express Highway at Kings Highway. He stopped his car and turned a spotlight on it. The creature circled for a moment or two, then streaked northward. "I've seen it three times in the last four days, and that's too much tomfoolery for a man of fifty to take," Bradford told the press.

Hertenstein's Heron

Apparently it was getting to be too much for other people as well, if the letters stacking up in the office of St. Louis Mayor Aloys P. Kaufmann were any indication. "Why has nothing been done about this?" one letter writer demanded to know. "All St. Louis is upset about it. Who knows? Maybe it's a man-killing bird." Another wrote, "I don't think it's a bird—but I hope it is." Still others offered theories: it was an albatross, a blue heron, a pelican—all unlikely "explanations" considering the reported behavior and size of the bird. The explanations, therefore, became as bizarre as the sightings themselves.

Officials were leaning over backwards to quiet the furor. The mayor, for his part, passed the buck to his administrative assistant, Charles Hertenstein, who was given instructions (apparently seriously) to set a trap for the beast. However, after discovering blue heron tracks on an island in the Meramec River on the thirtieth, Hertenstein, relieved, suggested this might be the explanation; although the reports had suggested a considerably larger bird than the blue heron, a common enough sight along the Illinois-Missouri border.

The Sightings Continue

The next day Hertenstein's sigh of relief had turned into a groan. "Don't tell me we now have a self-illuminated flying monster," he complained. But that is precisely what three St. Louis citizens, Charles Dunn, a U.S. Steel inspector, his wife Mary, and Clifford Warden, had reported seeing the night before at ten o'clock. Said Charles Dunn, "I thought people who reported the thing were seeing 'bugs' until I looked into the sky last night. It was flapping its wings and moving quite fast at about three thousand feet altitude and appeared to be illuminated by a dull glow. It looked about the size of a Piper Cub plane, but there was no engine sound, and it was not a plane. I could hardly believe my eyes."

At this juncture the Civil Air Patrol offered to make aerial searches for the bird whose appearances had begun to attract national attention. A man from Bowling Green, Indiana, wrote Hertenstein to tell him he had seen it or something very similar two years before, and it had been the size of a twelve-hundred-pound horse. Albert T. Bertram, Jr., a meteorological aide with the US Weather Bureau, describing his May 2nd sighting, said the bird resembled the storks he had seen in Africa

Then on May 5th, the glowing, giant bird paid its last 1948 visit to the St Louis-Alton area. Arthur Davidson, a candy broker of University City, Missouri, called the police at 9:05 PM to say he had seen it. He noted "it was greyish and illuminated...It seemed to be flying over the old folk's home." At 10:30 PM, Mrs. William Stallings of nearby St Louis informed the authorities that she and her husband had seen it. "It was bright, about as big as a house. It was greenish-yellow and bobbed up and down," Stallings said.

Ironically, just as the public excitement reached its peak, the sightings came to an abrupt end.

The Piasa and Kin

To the Native Americans of the area, the giant mystery birds were really nothing new. Their traditions are filled with stories about the Piasa. The French explorer Marquette was the first European to describe this legendary creature, for the Illini had left an artistic representation of it for all to see. Marquette wrote:

> On the flat face of a high rock were painted, in red, black, and green, a pair of monsters, each as large as a calf, with horns like a deer, red eyes, a beard like a tiger, and a frightful expression of countenance. The face is something like that of a man, the body covered with scales, and the tail so long that it passes entirely round the body, over the head, and between the legs, ending like that of a fish.

An Alton, Illinois scholar named McAdams, observed during the mid-1800s, that the name Piasa "signifies, in Illini, 'The bird which devours men.'" Some modern translators have simply recorded the meaning as "Giant Bird that Devours Man."

According to legend, the giant bird had its home high in a cave in the bluff. In the beginning, it was able to coexist with the Illini, but during a battle between two tribes, the Piasa carried away two warriors, feasted on them, and acquired a liking for human flesh. Soon children and adults were carried away and eaten. All Illini lived in fear. A brave named Massatoga devised a plan. He would stand and chant, acting as bait for the Piasa, while twenty of the bravest warriors hid in ambush. The scheme worked, and this Piasa was killed.

A painted re-creation of the original Piasa is today a local landmark. It can be seen on the bluff just north of Alton, Illinois, on the Great River Road. Late in the 1990s the Piasa, through the efforts of citizens, government, and business advocates, was repainted on the bluff and restored to its former pristine state. Stop by and see it sometime.

Among the Cherokee, the legend of the Tlanuwa is quite similar. On the north bank of the Little Tennessee River, in Blount County, Tennessee, is the cave of the Tlanuwa, immense birds who would fly up and down the valley. Often the giant birds would come into villages and pick up dogs and even small children. Eventually, a medicine man was approached and enlisted to rid the area of the Tlanuwa. He did so by killing the parent bird's young. Cherokee legend notes they were so furious they soared out of sight and were never seen again.

Or were they? When Amerindians living in the St. Louis-Alton area heard the white man's 1948 reports, they remembered the Piasa and other thunderbird accounts from their grandfathers and merely shook their heads.

Illinois' Big Birds of the '70s

The encounters with big birds in Illinois stretch through time from Marquette's notes of 1673 to the reports some three hundred years later. The most dramatic recent encounter happened in 1977, when two large birds swooped down and tried to pick up young Marlon Lowe. It was only the beginning of one of the biggest Thunderbird flaps to hit Illinois.

The Lawndale, Illinois, incident is among the most important avian cryptozoological events ever to have been investigated. It is a modern, real-life enactment of a kind of episode portrayed in folklore all over the world: the attempted abduction of a child by a Thunderbird.

On July 25, 1977, as 10-year-old Marlon Lowe played outside his family home along open fields near Kickapoo Creek, two giant birds passed over. One suddenly swooped down to grab the boy, carrying him a few feet before dropping him, apparently because of his frightened mother's screams. The huge birds let go of their sixty-pound cargo in front of the white-paneled trailer with black eagles on the shutters, then casually flew off toward the creek, flapping their way into history.

The Sheriff investigated, the media arrived, and so to did my brother, Jerry Coleman of Decatur, Illinois. He was able to interview Marlon and his parents Jake and Ruth Lowe within hours of the incident. Two years later, I joined him to conduct a follow-up interview. In 1996 Jerry Coleman, accompanied by a crew from Yorkshire Television, spoke again with Marlon and his mother.

"I'll always remember how that huge thing was bending its white ringed neck," Ruth Lowe remarked. It seemed to be trying to peck at Marlon as it was flying away. Though she compared the bird's size to an ostrich's, she said it looked more like a condor. After the incident she spent many hours in the library trying to identify the bird, without success. She rejected a local sheriff's speculation that it had been no more than a turkey vulture. "I was standing at the door, and all I saw was Marlon's feet dangling in the air," she recalled, adding the obvious: "There just aren't any birds around here that could lift him up like that."

Mark A. Hall, author of *Thunderbird: The Living Legend!* (1994), concludes an extended discussion of the Lawndale incident thusly: "The final word on the Illinois wonder deservedly goes to Ruth Lowe. After all the experts had their say, Mrs. Lowe, who spoke from personal experience, has made the most perceptive comment on the appearance of two extraordinary birds in Illinois. She was quoted as saying: 'The game warden said there wasn't anything like this ever reported in the county. Maybe there wasn't, but there is now. Two came through here last night.'"

And like others after them, all the witnesses of July 25th—Mr. Cox, Jack and Betty Daniels, Jake, Marlon, Jackie and Ruth Lowe, and Mike Thompson—described exactly the same thing: two huge coal, black birds with long, white-ringed necks, long curled beaks, and wingspans of ten or more feet.

Several others sightings followed on the heels of the Lawndale event. On 28 July 1977 Stanley Thompson, his wife, and several friends saw one of the big birds fly over their farm late in the day. They were all watching some radio controlled model airplanes when Mrs.Thompson said, "Look at that funny looking plane that guy's flying." Soon she yelled, "It's a bird!" and everyone turned to watch. Stan told the sheriffs police that the bird had a six-foot body and a wingspan of nine or ten feet. McLean County Sheriffs Sergeant Robert Boyd said Thompson "has been around here a long time. He's a credible witness. When I heard some of those earlier reports, I figured the people must be in the sauce. But these are responsible people. I've changed my mind, and we're going to investigate."

James Majors of Bloomington was the next witness. He was driving a mail truck from Armington to Delavan when he saw the birds. He said they had wingspans of over eight feet; plump bodies; straight tails; legs with claws for feet, about 2.5 to 3.5 feet long; pointed eight-inch-long bills; and mean/ugly looking faces. He saw one glide into a nearby field and pick up a small animal, apparently a pig. Majors continued to drive into town, stopped, jumped out, and quickly smoked four cigarettes to regain his composure. "I think what I saw is a giant, large condor," Majors remarked soon after his late July sighting,

Late on Thursday, July 28th, Lisa Montgomery, eighteen, of Tremont was washing her car when she looked up and saw a giant bird with at least a seven foot wingspan. "It was black, but I couldn't see its markings. It had a real low tail," she said. When it disappeared, it was flying toward Pekin, Illinois.

At 2:00 AM on Saturday, July 30th, Dennis Turner of Downs, Illinois and two of his friends saw a large bird with at least a six-foot wingspan perch on a telephone pole near the Gillum and Randolph Roads. Turner said the bird dropped something near the pole, and police later found a foot-long rat at the spot.

On the same day, Waynesville residents said they saw a large black bird with an eight-foot wingspan circling the area at about 2:00 PM.

Texas John Affair

The 1977 flap of the Illinois big birds was filling the papers daily, when the "Texas John" affair occurred. On Saturday, July 30th, John Huffer of Tuscola, Illinois, who was known locally as Texas John for reasons unknown, filmed what he says were the "big birds." Huffer, a some-times-writer for *Bass Magazine,* construction worker, former Marine combat photographer, and an infrequent freelance television filmmaker, was out fishing with his son that hot July morning in 1977 when he saw the birds. Huffer said the two birds deposited baseball-sized droppings around a dead tree in which they had roosted. Huffer then scared them with his boat horn and commenced filming. After getting more than one hundred feet of film of the two large birds, Huffer approached Champaign's WCIA-TV station and sold them part of the film for one newscast. He said the biggest bird's head was eighteen inches long and that its wingspan spread twelve feet.

Then things started getting a little bizarre. First there were the mis-quotes. For example, Huffer had observed, regarding the larger of the two birds: "I weigh 260 pounds, and I didn't want to get too close to it." By the time some wire services in this country and in England got the story, Huffer was quoted as saying the big bird had weighed 260 pounds!

Soon thereafter Huffer sold the description (yes, the *description*) of the big bird, according to a statement he made to me in December of 1977, "it is now (the) property of Reader's Digest." He also tried to arrange the sale of the film to Sun Classics. By February 1979 he was signing his letters "John Huffer, The Native American Outdoor Writer" and asking for my assistance in disorganized letters: "Help. *Reader's Digest* is holding the real Big Bird story because I am an Indian," Huffer wrote. "We do not feel this is right. Please write to...," and then he would forward me the name of yet another contact.

The matter of Texas John or "Indian John" (as he was calling him-self in 1979) distracted the press from the other straightforward reports of the big birds. By the time the Huffer story had hit the papers, the early Lowe/Lawndale abduction attempt was tacked on at the end of news account merely as "rumors and tales of birds kidnapping children."

The showing of the color film allowed the experts to quickly identify Huffer's birds as turkey vultures, and then label all the big birds seen as turkey vultures. Jack Ellis, supervisor of Wildlife Resources for Illinois' Department of Conservation, issued a statement to the press that he had seen the film and the case was closed on all the nonsense about big birds. William K. Beecher, director of the Chicago Academy of Sciences, said, "What we're seeing is a lot of hysteria, maybe some funning like the kangaroo stories we had a while back, " referring to creatures seen throughout the U.S.A. since the 1800s by police officers, housewives, and scores of other credible witnesses. (See chapter 14, "Mystery Kangaroos" in *Mysterious America*.)

The whole Texas John affair was a strange one. But if the attack by the experts on the big birds helped put into motion what we tend to call the "ridicule factor," the word must have not reached the birds. The sightings continued, though the end was in sight.

Mrs. Albert Dunham, of rural Bloomington, was sitting in the second floor of her home at about 4:00 PM on Sunday, July 31st, when she noticed a shadow passing outside over her house. First, she assumed the shadow was of a cloud, but when she glanced quickly up, she viewed what she thought was a small plane. Then she took a good, hard look and was shocked to realize it was really a big bird. "I've had my doubts about the reports, I really did," Mrs. Dunham said. "I wondered if I was just seeing something because of all the publicity." But she quickly realized something unusual was flying overhead. "It was twenty feet directly above me and I could pick out the underneath details very well. It was black with a white ring around its neck and white on its fanlike tail," she said. "It has a long straight bill and is a great big, huge bird." Her son chased it to a nearby landfill, but it vanished before a local newspaper's photographer could take a picture.

The Experts and the Air Force

The last of the publicly reported series of big bird sightings occurred on Thursday, August 11, 1977, in southwestern Illinois, near Odin. John and Wanda Chappell were the last witnesses to come forward. They said they had seen a great, gray bird with a twelve-foot wingspan and six-foot long body. "It was so big it had a hard time finding a limb big enough to land on," John Chappel remarked. His wife said, "It looked like a prehistoric bird. It was really fantastic. It was big enough to lift something. Our daughter is a year and a half old and it was big enough to lift a child bigger than her. It was that huge." In a hint of what people who were seeing the bird must have been feeling at this juncture of the flap, Wanda Chappell said, "We were hesitant to report it because we thought people might think we were exaggerating, but then I called my sister Alma. She said it was also sighted yesterday, so we thought if we reported it someone else might see it." If it was seen again in Illinois in 1977, no one told the police or press.

The notion that the big birds were only turkey vultures, despite the fact turkey vultures have bright, distinctive red heads and a wingspan of less than six feet, was being widely reported in the papers. Why would witnesses dare have their names printed under headlines that read: "Experts Talk Turkey on Big Bird Story!" ? The sightings, if they continued, was a dead story for the papers.

Yet the big bird sightings did continue, informally exchanged between local people who were interested in the subject. When I visited the Lowes in 1979, I was told of encounters that had occurred up to that time but were kept quiet because of the ridicule curtain (i.e. fear of public harassment).

Even the United States Air Force took note of the Illinois big bird stories. According to John Keel, Jacques Vallee, the famed French computer authority and ufologist who served as the model for the role played by Francois Truffaut in *Close Encounters of the Third Kind*, was given access to the Air Force UFO files and found a curious big bird story among them. The report said an Air Force colonel was driving along an Illinois road one night (date not given) when he became aware of a huge bird the size of a small airplane directly overhead. It flapped its massive wings and soared away.

Modern Accounts
People continue to send me big bird sightings. Illustrating the modern diversity of sightings, Allison Jornlin of Milwaukee, Wisconsin, recorded what has become known as the "The Brookfield Thunderbird" incident. It happened during the late afternoon of September 21, 1988.

Kevin, the twenty-five year old witness, a police science degree holder and future Gulf War veteran, was staring out the ten-foot bay windows on an upper floor of Brookfield's Elmbrook Memorial Hospital. He was alone, pacing the room, awaiting the birth of his first child. Looking out a hospital window, from high on the bluff, he had a magnificent view of the surrounding countryside. Suddenly a black form dipping in and out of the clouds caught his attention. If it was an airplane, it meant trouble, because it was flying dangerously low. Kevin stopped pacing to track the object's flight. A full animate object suddenly emerged from dense clouds. Startled, Kevin realized that it wasn't an airplane. It looked very much like a large bird.

"I wanted to run out of the room, but I couldn't move," he told investigator Jornlin. Whatever it was, "it was bigger than a full-size pickup truck, but smaller than a Piper Cub plane."

The enormous creature continued sailing closer, noted Jornlin's report. It did not flap its wings, but glided on air currents, always just underneath the clouds, as if "using them for cover." Kevin estimated that the creature's wingspan was 12 to 15 feet across, with a similar span from its head to the tip of its tail. It glided in clear view for about a minute, coming within 100 yards of the hospital windows. Kevin started to call out to attract the attention of others, so that they could verify what he was seeing, but he froze when he felt as if the creature had sensed his presence.

"At some point, I was aware that it was aware of me," he says. Immobilized, he watched as the enormous creature turned its head, locking in on him standing exposed behind the broad sheet of glass. Then, as if knowing it had been spotted, the creature suddenly soared back into the covering clouds. Kevin could only shake his head, thinking, "Could I really be stressed out enough to have imagined this?....I've never had any other type of weird experience and I wasn't under any real duress at the time," he says.

Perhaps there was a flap taking place in 1988, because I received another Thunderbird report for this time period. T. Stewart's sighting took place in Minnesota, at Pryor Lake, not far from the Minnesota horse and hunt club. In her own words, here's what happened:

When I saw the bird I was on a return trip from Canada. My father (a Chesapeake Bay retriever trainer and breeder) ran a few of his dogs in a Canadian field trail. And we were in Minnesota because he was to be a judge at the Minnesota horse and hunt club's field trials. We found a trailer park on lake Pryor in mid-morning. I took one of the dogs (Katie) to have a look around, and to find out where the restrooms were located. They were right across from the lake, where I saw 7-9 adults playing on a raft at the water's edge.

The next morning just after sunrise I woke up and headed to the restrooms, taking Katie with me. On exiting the restroom I noticed the dog staring at the lake and not responding to me. I looked over at the water, which was about 20-25 feet from where I stood. I saw the biggest bird I've ever seen in my life standing on the raft I had seen the day before. It was standing where I could see it's left side and it was looking in the direction of the dog and me. The dog then whined and ran off leaving me there alone.

I stared at the bird for quite some time, afraid to move. It was between 7-8 feet in height (judging by the height of the men I'd seen on the raft the day before). It had dark brown feathers on the body and white to off-white feathers at the neck area. Its feet were similar to feet I've seen on hawks.

It had been looking in my direction the whole time that I stood there, and then it spread it's wings and flew off over the lake, I watched till I could no longer see it. I then went back to the camper where I found the dog Katie under the camper whining.

I live in southeast Wisconsin and I've seen many birds in my area and had never seen any that looked even remotely like what I saw that day. We have eagles, hawks, herons, and loons and this bird was many, many times bigger then any of the birds I've seen. The wingspan had to be more then twice the size of its body. When it took off it flapped its wings no more then 6-9 times then glided over the lake and into the surrounding woods. This happened in either late July to early August. The dog was a trained hunting dog and has protected me from many predators in the woods. I've never seen her scared of anything till that time.

In recent years, speculation has it that the 1948 incidents were an indication of one track of the migration path of these birds as they flew from the Ozarks up to the northern reaches of their range. Another migration path appears to be in the eastern sections of Appalachia, and involves everything from the Mothman accounts of the 1960s to the old sightings from the Black Forest of Pennsylvania, as well as the newest encounters from the area.

Black Forest of Pennsylvania

One apparent "window" region for Thunderbird events has been the Black Forest. Known also as the Forbidden Land, the Pennsylvania Black Forest region encompasses Cameron, Clinton, Potter, Lycoming, Tioga, and McKean counties. It's mostly rural, little populated state forest and wildlife lands. The earliest known sightings of Thunderbirds here date back to the 1840s, and are chronicled by Robert Lyman, Sr., in his booklet, *Amazing Indeed: Strange Events in the Black Forest,* volume two. Other researchers such as Mark A. Hall, Stan Gordon, and Gerald Musinsky have tracked this series of Thunderbird events.

Indeed, historian Robert Lyman, Sr., interviewed by Hall a year before Lyman's death in 1974, spoke of "thunderbird flocks" which frequented the Dent's Run area in 1892. In April 1922, Hiram Crammer saw his first Thunderbird with a 35 foot wing spread at Hammersley Fork. In 1957, Cramer and Lyman told of Thunderbirds being seen regularly over Renovo, Westport, Shintown, and Hammersley Fork. Near Bush Dam in 1964, road workers watched a Thunderbird carry off a fawn.

Hall's history of all the old sightings shows a good record of accounts from the 1800s onward. Musinsky has reviewed these accounts further and adds detailed encounters down through the years, near Mt. Zion Church cemetery, south of a marsh near State Game Lands No. 252 and

North White Deer Ridge in Lycoming County, in 1989; near Hyner, in Clinton County in September, 1992; and near Larry's Creek in July 1993.

This is clearly an active area.

Pennsylvania Events: 2001

Pennsylvania has continued its long history of sightings, and during 2001, a series occurred in the southwestern part of the state late in September. Researcher Stan Gordon forwarded this initial report from just north of West Virginia:

> A 19-year-old witness [Mike Felice] claims to have seen a huge bird in South Greensburg, located in Westmoreland County, Pennsylvania...on Tuesday evening, September 25, 2001. I conducted an in-depth interview with the witness by phone. On Thursday, Dennis Smeltzer, an associate researcher with a serious interest in ornithology, went to the location of the sighting, and interviewed the witness.
>
> The sighting occurred at about 7:30 PM local time, when it was beginning to turn dark. The witness was outside at the time, and was close to Route 119, which is a major highway. The witness was observing the trucks and cars passing by when his attention was drawn upwards by a sound "like flags flapping in a thunderstorm." He observed a huge bird which appeared to be black, or very dark grayish-brown. The witness was startled at the wingspan of the creature, which he estimated to be between 10 and 15 feet.
>
> The bird's head was estimated to be about 3 feet long, about as large as a small dog. When the bird was first observed, the witness stated, "I wouldn't say it was flapping it's wings gracefully, but almost horrifically flapping it's wings very slowly, then gliding above the passing big rig trucks." The creature seemed to be following the truck traffic, passing overhead at about 50 to 60 feet.
>
> The bird flew about 150 feet down the road towards a wooded area. The bird spread it's wings, showing the witness

how massive it was, as it swooped down on a dead tree near a billboard. This fellow continued to watch as it dropped slowly, yet forcefully, and saw the bird ruffle its feathers, and saw its head move around. After several seconds the bird rose from the tree, and gave the man the impression that the tree would bow and break from the apparent weight. The bird then flew out of view towards another wooded area. The entire sighting lasted around a minute and a half. Immediately after the occurrence, this man ran to a local business to ask if anyone saw what he observed. He also approached a woman who was nearby, but she didn't see it either. The witness was upset that apparently no one else had reported this creature.

Smeltzer looked around the area of the tree where the bird was reported to have landed, but no evidence could be found. It's Smeltzer's impression that the witness is not fabricating and is describing to the best of his ability what he observed. The witness appears familiar with the great blue heron, vulture, and eagle, and is certain that this is not what he saw.

Soon, Stan Gordon, myself, and others became aware of similar Pennsylvania Thunderbird reports. As result of the above report on a possible Thunderbird sighting, Craig Heinselman, cryptozoologist and editor of *Crypto*, told me that he had received information on three other possible Thunderbird sightings from the Keystone state that appeared to demonstrate a broader recent pattern of sightings.

On June 13, 2001, a resident of the town of Greenville, Pennsylvania reported seeing a large bird the size of a small airplane from his living room. Greensville is a small town that lies near the border of Ohio and about halfway between Erie and Pittsburgh. The witness, Ray, upon further inquiry during a phone interview with Craig Heinselman on June 15, 2001, was able to flesh out the original report. Ray described the bird as fully feathered and dark brown or black color. The back of the wings was a grayish-black. Its body was not bulky and the overall appearance was not like any bird he had ever seen. As the house lies near Little Shedango Stream and the house overlooks a small pond and woodlands, Ray was extremely familiar with the birds and other wildlife in the area including bald eagles, vultures and storks. Ray stated that the bird flew in from the south at a distance of 200-300 yards from the window and landed on a large tree beside the small pond. As it flew in, he saw a shadow first and thought it was an ultra light aircraft, which are used in the area by some neighbors. The bird landed and remained on the tree for 15-to-20 minutes, and then took off again to the south. Ray estimated that the wingspan was equivalent to some of the ultra lights he has seen in the area, around 15 feet of wingspan and upwards of five feet of body size.

During the interview Ray made a passing mention as well of a neighbor who, although not familiar with the area wildlife, reported to Ray's wife about a large bird she had seen on June 14, 2001. The bird was described as "the biggest bird I ever saw" and bigger than a stork. Again the bird was "a blackish color."

The third report comes out of Erie County from July 6, 2001. It came to Heinselman's attention from a letter printed in the UK-based magazine *Fortean Times*. Robin Swope, the witness, reported a large bird flying near a Greenville area mausoleum as she cut the grass. It flew by some high tension wires and was estimated to be 15-to-17 feet in wingspan." It was described as: "...dark grey with little or no neck, and a circle of black under it's head. Its beak was very thin and long, about a foot in length...."

An Underlying Pattern?

Needless to say, these big bird sightings are not an isolated series of encounters. Specific areas across the nation tend to have their histories of sightings. My files on the subject literally overflow. For example, the Black Forest region near Coudersport, Pennsylvania has a chain of incidents dating from the 1890s into the 2000s. I have articles and letters from folks in the Ozarks telling of Thunderbirds carrying off kids and livestock from post-Civil War times until the present. The series of New Jersey Devil accounts from the early 1900s and the Mothman sightings in Ohio and West Virginia in the 1960s both contain elements of the big birds' behavioral patterns, although both no doubt are admixtures of other cryptozoological and Fortean items.

Making sense of this mass of tales, legends, sightings, and encounters is not an easy task. Amerindian folklore and backwoods knowledge appear to be the smoke above some interesting fires, but the lack of hard facts and details make it difficult to pin the stories on specific specimens of birds. The more recent accounts sometimes are misidentifications of known birds. I have not included all of the reports I have from very well meaning people .of what were actually found to be hawks, eagles, blue herons, or even peahens. Texas John Huffer's sighting over Lake Shelbyville, furthermore, could very well be a couple of turkey vultures. In any series of sightings, I frequently sort through and discard some sightings that are, no doubt, rare but common enough birds. In the Illinois cases given in this chapter, for example, I am certain a few of those stories are exaggerations of turkey vultures and other infrequently seen Illinois birds.

There remains, nevertheless, a hard core of sightings from Illinois and along the Ohio River Valley, from Appalachia and the Ozarks, from Utah, Nevada, California, Oklahoma, and Texas, of large dark birds with wingspans of ten to sixteen feet that carry off animals and attempt to abduct children.

Are Condors to Blame?

What could these birds be? They seem to have something to do with the largest known soaring birds presently accepted by ornithologists—the condors. So let's take a look at these birds. The Andean condor, *Vultur gryphus*, lives from seven thousand to sixteen thousand feet up in the Andes, from Columbia south to Tierra del Fuego. It is the world's largest flying bird, with a wingspan of about ten feet, which can reach twelve feet in some specimens. The Andean condor is glossy black with white upper wing coverts, a baldhead, and a white collar of feathers around its neck. They are known to attack and kill sick and small animals for food, although their primary source of meals is carrion, dead animals like deer, horses, sheep, and rabbits. Most bird experts state that the feet of this condor and its North American cousin are too weak to carry food for moderately far distances.

The California condor, *Gymnogyps californianus*, is smaller than the Andean condor. However, with a nine-foot wingspan, it is the largest flying bird in North America. The California condor is sooty black and lacks the white neck collar. (The 1977 series of Illinois big birds reportedly had white neck feathers, which would mean they were closer in appearance to the Andean condor than to the California.) The present range of the 30 or so wild-released California condors (which obviously are close to extinction) is restricted to southern California and Arizona. Until recently, this condor lived throughout the extreme West, and in the early 1800s it lived in the East, according to Halliday's *Vanishing Birds*. When California condors were more numerous they seemed to have moved around a lot more than they do now. In his 1958 book, *Extinct and Vanishing Birds of the World*, James C. Greenway, Jr. observed: "In the past, a hundred and more years ago, there may have been a seasonal movement of population. This would account for the appearance of the birds near the Columbia River in Oregon in certain seasons." Greenway notes that there used to be "great congregations of birds in the autumn, particularly where food was plentiful."

Stepping back from the recent reports of big birds, a pattern of appearances does form. In late March, early April, and during July and August, from the Ozarks, down the Ohio River Valley, into the Appalachian Mountains, an irregular migration of the big birds seems to occur. Some of the Appalachian accounts of the Mothman are probably of Thunderbirds, as witnesses may have been watching the skies closely and reporting everything. The appearances in the western mountain states also seem natural. Considering their appearance, behavior, flight patterns, and size, could our big birds actually be condors? Are the nearly extinct California condors flying about the Midwest scaring the daylights out of people? Probably not. The existing condors are being closely watched. In addition, the big birds are larger than the California condors. And last but not least, the big birds appear to be so much more aggressive than the condors.

But I think that a near relative of the condor may be responsible for the big bird sightings. This relative may still be found in the wilderness craggies of the Bald Mountains that the Amerinds tell us are inhabited by thunderbirds and in the sheer cliff caves of the Smokies and Ozarks where backwoods people still tell of meetings with giant birds. Despite the interstates and jetports, those hilly outposts of nature do exist, and the big birds are calling them home.

The Terrible Teratorns

The candidate most in line with the big birds are the supposedly recently extinct teratorns. Alan Feduccia in *The Age of Birds* sums them up this way: "Perhaps the most remarkable of the Ice Age vulturine birds found in the New World were the teratorns....The very common *Teratornis merriami* had a wing span of 11 to 12 feet, and *Teratornis incredibilis,* known from Pleistocene deposits in Nevada and California, had a wing span that may have approached 17 feet. But the real giant was an Argentine fossil, nearly twice the size of *Teratornis merriami,* stood 5 feet tall and had a wing span of about 24 feet; it is the largest flying bird known to science."

Kenneth E. Campbell, one of the discoverers of the Argentine giant, has long studied the teratorns and disagrees with the usual assumption that they, like condors, were carrion eaters. Campbell has noted: "The long, narrow hooked beak and the type of mechanism found in this species are similar to those that grabbed small animals with its beak and swallowed them whole." Campbell senses they were predators, based upon his investigation of *Teratornis merriami,* which are so numerous at the La Brea tar pits.

Indeed, the only find of human remains at the La Brea tar pits occurs where the bones of teratorns were also found. John C. Merriam, writing in *Science* in August 1914, reported on the digging in pit number ten at La Brea: "The most interesting discovery was the finding on February 5 [1914] of an upper jaw from a human skull....Careful investigation of this vent disclosed later almost the entire skull with portions of the skeleton. The remains evidently belonged to one [middle-aged female] individual....The only extinct form certainly recognized in the material...is *Teratornis,* a gigantic condor-like bird, as yet known only from Rancho La Brea...Bones of this bird were found...above some of

---

the human remains. As nearly as one can judge from the evidence at hand, there seems a reasonable chance that the giant *Teratornis* was a contemporary of the human being whose remains appear in the north chimney of pit ten. The evidence does not present clear proof in favor of this view, but appears to balance in that direction."

The bones of the teratorns have since turned up in deposits from California to Florida, and it thus appears they were found throughout the United States of America, as well as the northern parts of Mexico. This distribution fits nicely with the reports of the big birds. Furthermore, the bones, some as recent as eight thousand years old, have almost always been found in conjunction with human habitation sites. Were the Amerindians killing these condor like birds for their feathers or because the birds had been kidnapping their stock and children?

Did the teratorns look like our big birds? Interestingly, *National Geographic* and other official efforts to represent the teratorns have shown them as very condor like with white ruffs around their neck, obviously modeling them after the Andean, not the California, condor. Still, as with most fossil remains, we really don't know what the teratorns looked like.

The long list of big bird sightings I have collected over the years may have to be reexamined someday by ornithologists. Right now, if you read their literature closely, you will find scholarly pieces on the possible "last sightings" of condors in Arizona's Yuma County in 1934 or a "questionable sighting recorded from Utah" in 1874. If a teratorn were caught in the near future, these same scientists would have to seriously reconsider to all the reports of big birds, from those of Logan County, Illinois to the account of a Piper Cub-sized bird viewed over Logan Street, Salt Lake City.

It might even force them to rethink those more birdlike Mothman encounters.

CHAPTER 5

Lizardmen

Chapter Ten of John A. Keel's *Strange Creatures from Time and Space* is devoted entirely to a hodgepodge of mostly American beasts Keel felt were related in some way to the Abominable Snowman and Bigfoot. These ape-like monsters, said to be roaming the "hollers and hills" of the eastern and southern United States, have always been a focus of my fieldwork research efforts, and one third of Keel's cases for his chapter actually came from my files. When I picked up the book in the 1970s and read it for the first time, something about Keel's grouping made me feel uncomfortable. Finally, it dawned on me that Keel's chapter title was really not quite right. His title, "Creatures from the Black Lagoon," was a very catchy Keelian way of noting something strange was slithering through the swamps, but the original movie monster he had used as the model was anything but ape-like.

The eponymous Creature from the Black Lagoon was a reptilian "Lizardman," a bipedal, human-sized beast that looked more like a spiny skinned were-lizard than a hairy were-gorilla or werewolf. The thing was literally a half-man, half-amphibious reptile.

Now, as creatures go, these types of monsters are rare, but by no means nonexistent. A lot of monster lumping does occur by Forteans and cryptozoologists, so my task was to closely examine the accounts of existing creatures, whether called Bigfoot, swamp monsters, or whatever, to reveal the true Creatures from the Black Lagoon, the Lizardmen.

West Coast Cases
The confusion between various uncommon cases comes into focus when you examine the history of one classic so-called "Bigfoot" story, the Wetzel-Riverside, California sighting of the fall of 1958. The Riverside

sighting entered public awareness so soon after the Bluff Creek, California original "Bigfoot" print find by Jerry Crew in October 1958, that it has naturally been retold often in Sasquatch books. In 1982, I tracked down and interviewed Charles Wetzel and his family personally, coming up with some interesting new information.

Wetzel, born July 8, 1934, was driving his green, two-door 1952 Buick Super near Riverside, California, when he saw "it." Saturday, November 8, 1958, is a night Charlie would not soon forget. He even remembers which radio station (KFI in Los Angeles) he had tuned into that night. Wetzel neared the part of North Main Street where the Santa Ana River infrequently overflows its banks, and sure enough, at a spot where the road dips, water was rushing across the pavement. So Charles slowed down. Within moments he was struck by two sensory events, which caught him off guard. First, his car radio started to transmit lots of static. He changed stations, he told me, but to no avail. Next, he saw what he thought was a temporary danger sign near the flooded site. Before he could think twice about any of this, Charles Wetzel saw a six-foot creature bound across his field of vision and stop in front of his Buick. The creature had a "round, scarecrowish head like something out of Halloween," Wetzel said at the time. He described it then, and to me later, as having no ears; no nose; a beak-like, protuberant mouth; and fluorescent, shining eyes. The skin was "scaly, like leaves, but definitely not feathers," Wetzel recalled during our 1982 talk.

The creature was waving "sort of funny" with its incredibly long arms, and seemed to be walking from the hips, almost as if it had no knees. Wetzel then remembered another detail not noted at the time: the legs stuck out from the sides of the torso, not from the bottom. The gurgling sounds it made were mixed with high-pitched screams. When it saw Wetzel it reached across the hood and began clawing at the windshield. Terrified, Wetzel grabbed the .22 High Standard pistol he kept in the car because he was often on the road at night. Clutching the gun, the frightened Californian stomped on the gas. "Screeching like a f——r," as Wetzel graphically put it, the creature tumbled forward off the hood and was run over by the car. Wetzel could hear it scrape the pan under the engine, and later police lab tests revealed that something had indeed scrubbed the grease from the Buick's underside.

The police used bloodhounds to search the area, but the dogs found nothing and the officers were left with only the sweeping claw marks on Wetzel's windshield to ponder. Then, the very next night, a black something jumped out of the underbrush near the same site and frightened another motorist. In recent years, sightings of the strange three-toed Bigfoot have been reported from surrounding areas of southern California, notably the smelly eight-footer seen emerging from a drainage ditch in Buena Park in May, 1982.

Clearly the Wetzel creature fits the reptilian mold better than the anthropoid. A thing with fluorescent eyes, a protuberant mouth, and a body covered with scales certainly doesn't sound like a Sasquatch.

The connection to water is a strong theme in all of these Lizardmen accounts so it is not so surprising that the next piece of the puzzle comes from the lake monster file. Trekking up the west coast, the following report concerns a monster that actually looks like it stepped out of the wardrobe room of the Black Lagoon movie.

Thetis Lake, a small manmade reservoir near Colwood, British Columbia, is not far from Victoria. Cadboro Bay, off Victoria and Vancouver Island, is well known for the perennial sea monster "Cadborosaurus," so understandably a new creature in the neighborhood would be grouped under the same facade by the press. But the Thetis Lake Monster appears to be something else altogether.

On August 19, 1972 Gordon Pike and Robin Flewellyn said a five-foot-tall animal appeared on the surface of Thetis Lake and chased them from the beach. Flewellyn was cut on the hand by six razor-sharp points atop the monster's head. A Royal Canadian Mounted Police (RCMP) officer was quoted at the time as saying "The boys seem sincere, and until we determine otherwise we have no alternative but to continue our investigation."

The next Wednesday afternoon, August 23rd, the Thetis Monster was encountered again. Mike Gold and Russell Van Nice said they saw "it" around 3:30 PM on the other side of the lake away from the recreation area of its first appearance. Mike Gold noted: "It came out of the water and looked around. Then it went back in the water. Then we ran!"

He described the creature as "shaped like an ordinary body, like a human being body but it had a monster face, and it was all scaly [with] a point sticking out its head [and] great big ears. It was silver."

At last word, the RCMP were investigating the Thetis Monster "because it's been reported to us, and we have to check these things out."

A similar creature has been reported in nearby Puget Sound in Washington. The Kwakiutl Indian merman, *Pugwis*, is sort of a cross between Sasquatch and the Creature from the Black Lagoon. Its fish-like face and paired incisors make this undersea spirit a prominent figure in Indian legend and is easily recognized in wood-carved art.

On To the Great Lakes

The Thetis Monster also resembles one seen in Saginaw, Michigan, which occurred in 1937. A man-like monster climbed up a river bank, leaned against a tree, and then returned to the river. The fisherman who witnessed this appearance suffered a nervous breakdown. This Saginaw tale, the reports of clawed and three-toed prints from Wisconsin to Missouri, and other supposedly "Bigfoot" or "manimal" encounters perhaps should be reexamined in light of the reptilian Creatures from the Black Lagoon.

The big Deltox Swamp, Wisconsin flap investigated by Ivan T. Sanderson in 1969, for example, has always been shelved with Bigfoot reports. But what are we to make of the tracks of the creature, which were said to be like footprints of "a good-sized man with swim fins"?

This trait is more frequently reported in the so-called eastern Bigfoot reports than most people realize. For example, there's the case of the Charles Mill Lake creature of Mansfield, Ohio, where I visited and re-interviewed locals in 1975. A green-eyed, seven-foot, seemingly armless humanoid was seen late in March 1959 by Michael Lane, Wayne Armstrong, and Dennis Patterson. It came out of the lake and left behind "tracks that resembled the footgear worn by skin divers." The thing was seen again in 1963 and described as "luminous and green-eyed." My examination of the site of these encounters demonstrated the Charles Mill Lake's swampy affinities—certainly a good home for a Black Lagoon beast.

In the annals of midwestern monster hunters is a cryptic chapter few discuss as they talk about the fieldwork done at Louisiana, Missouri. In the early 1970s, many folks looked into the widespread reports of "Momo" (Missouri Monster). One investigator was traveling down a back road and was surprised to see what appeared to be a grown man dressed in complete skin diving gear down to the swimfins, miles from any logical skindiving site. Does this report of a "frogman" have something to do with our inquiry?

Or what are we to make of reports of some "things" merging from Mothman-like beasts into the Creatures from the Black Lagoon? In Wisconsin, for example, there is the 1990s story of the "Reptile Man" of Highway 13, gathered by R. W. Wolff and posted by Fortean researcher Richard Hendricks on his Weird Wisconsin website (www.weird-wi.com). The highway goes north to south, down the middle of the state. A Department of Natural Resources warden was traveling down 13, south of Medford, Wisconsin, when suddenly he saw a figure standing in the middle of the road. It was hominoid, and about the same size of a human, but it appeared to be green-scaled. Incredibly, as the warden grew closer to the thing, he saw wings pop from the beast's back. Suddenly, it went straight up and flew over his vehicle, coming down and landing behind him. Later, the warden discovered that he wasn't the only person to have seen this thing. He learned that some highway workers had an almost identical experience along this same section of 13.

Though this quest is pulling us to the U.S. Midwest, the focus of the accounts, let's deal first with matters in New Jersey and New York.

Mid-Atlantic Swamps

You can take the reports, tales, and sightings of Creatures from the Black Lagoon and draw a continuous watery line down the Susquehanna River through the so-called Southern Tier of New York State, into the Tamarack swamps along the Delaware ending in the counties of Morris and Sussex in New Jersey. During the summer of 1973, residents of the Newton-Lafayette area in New Jersey described a giant, man-like alligator they had seen locally. Newspaper reporters wrote about an old Indian tale from the region that told of a giant, man-sized fish that could never be caught. In 1977, New York State Conservation Naturalist Alfred Hulstruck reported that the state's southern tier had "a scaled, man-like creature (that) appears at dusk from the red, algae-ridden waters to forage among the fern and moss-covered uplands."

The Ohio River Valley

The New York-New Jersey record for such creatures is minor and cannot compare with the overwhelming series of narratives issuing from the Ohio River Valley.

During the 1960s and 1970s, I dug into the back issues of the Louisville, Kentucky, *Courier-Journal* and discovered a gem that has kept me pondering its meaning for decades. The interesting little item appeared in the October 24, 1878 issue. A "Wild Man of the Woods" was captured, allegedly, in Tennessee, and then placed on exhibit in Louisville. The creature was described as being six feet, five inches tall, and having eyes twice the normal size. His body was "covered with fish scales." This 1878 article makes some sense in the context of these Lizardmen, if it wasn't some unfortunate individual with a skin abnormality.

Almost a hundred years later, again near Louisville, there are more stories of reptilian entities. In October 1975, near Milton, Kentucky, Clarence Cable reported that a "giant lizard" was roaming the forests near his automobile junkyard. Anomalist author Peter Guttilla described the creature Cable surprised as "about fifteen feet long, [with] a foot-long forked tongue, and big eyes that bulged something like a frog's. It was dull-white with black-and-white stripes across its body with quarter-size speckles over it."

On-site field investigations by Mark A. Hall, however, indicated this "giant lizard" ran bipedally, according to descriptions given by other Trimble County, Kentucky witnesses. The Ohio River is Louisville's, Milton and Trimble counties' northern boundary.

On August 21, 1955, near Evansville, Indiana, Mrs. Darwin Johnson was almost pulled forever into the depths of the Ohio River. In what seems to have been a very close meeting with one of these creatures, Mrs. Johnson, of Dogtown, Indiana, was swimming with her friend Mrs. Chris Lamble about fifteen feet from shore when suddenly something grabbed her from under the surface. It felt like the "hand " had huge claws and "furry" (or scaly?) palms. It came up from behind her, grabbed her left leg, gripped her knee, and pulled her under. She kicked and fought herself free. It pulled her under again. Although both women could not see the thing, they were screaming and yelling to scare it away. Finally, Mrs. Johnson lunged for Mrs. Lamble's inner tube, and the loud "thump" apparently scared "it" away, as "it" released its grip. Back on shore, Mrs. Johnson received treatment for her scratches and marks on her leg. Fortean investigator Terry Colvin passed on the information that Mrs. Johnson had a palm-print-shaped green stain below her knee that could not be removed for several days.

Interestingly, Colvin learned that an individual who identified himself as an Air Force colonel visited the Johnsons. He took voluminous notes and warned them not to talk further about the incident. Of course, this sounds very similar to a "Man-In-Black" encounter.

For anyone who has seen the film *The Creature from the Black Lagoon*, the Ohio River encounter of Mrs. Darwin Johnson is already familiar, for her attack was foreshadowed in that movie. John Baxter in his *Science Fiction in the Cinema*, recounts those moments: "A key scene of the film is when the heroine (Julie Adams) enters the water for a swim, unaware that the creature is swimming just below her, admiring. Shots looking up towards the surface show the girl penetrating a Cocteau-like mirror, her white suit with its accentuated breasts, her choreographed leg movements all overtly sexual. Gliding beneath her, twisting lasciviously in a stylized representation of sexual intercourse, the creature, his movements brutally masculine and powerful, contemplates his ritual bride, though his passion does not reach its peak until the girl performs some underwater ballet movements, explicitly erotic poses that excite the Gill-Man to reach out and clutch at her murmuring legs."

The cinematic Lizardman, the first Creature of the Black Lagoon, is presented in the film, according to Baxter, "As a force of elemental power, not maliciously evil but 'other-directed,' a fragment of a world where our ideas of morality have no relevance."

We can only speculate that the same may be true of the very "real" Creatures from the Black Lagoon.

Loveland's Trolls and Frogman

From Evansville, Indiana's watery attack to Loveland, Ohio's case of the "trolls under the bridge," the story continues along the Ohio River Valley, just down the river from Point Pleasant and Mothman country.

Leonard H. Stringfield's inquiry into the "affair under the bridge" is perhaps well known to most readers of ufology, but not to many others. The sighting occurred one day in March of 1955 at 4:00 AM in Branch Hill, Ohio. Robert Hunnicutt, a businessman, saw three manlike "trolls" kneeling on the side of the road. They were about three feet tall, had gray skin, and seemed to be wearing tight-fitting gray clothes or have skin that appeared so. They had froglike faces, long slender arms, normal eyes, but no eyebrows. One of them held a dark object (emitting blue flashes) between its raised arms. Hunnicutt tried to approach them but "must have lost consciousness," because he found himself driving to the police station without remembering what took place in the meantime. An FBI investigation followed and a guard was placed on the bridge.

Clearly some weird things were going on in the region at the time. On August 25, 1955, near Greenhills, Ohio, four adolescents in an automobile saw a luminous creature standing near a fireplug, according to Stringfield. And six weeks earlier, on July 3, 1955, in Stockton, Georgia, Mrs. Wesley Symmonds was driving near this town when she saw four "bug-eyed" creatures near the road. They were small beings with thin arms, large eyes, and pointed chins. Two were turned away from the witness; one was bending over with something like a stick in its hand; and the fourth was facing her with its right arm raised. It had bulging eyes, a sort of cap, no visible mouth, a long pointed nose, a chin which came to a sharp point, and long thin arms with claws.

The famed Kelly Creatures case, often mislabeled as the Hopkinsville, Kentucky Incident, took place during this same time frame, on August 21-22, 1955. The Sutton family and their relatives had to deal with a literal invasion of three feet tall "goblins" that glowed silver, had big eyes, and oversized heads. The things were hit by gunfire by the rural folks who were scared but firm in their resistance. The "goblins" merely floated away when shot.

The 1955 incidents in Indiana, Georgia, and Kentucky seem to be less isolated when put in the context of what was happening in Ohio in 1955. But there is one point I would like to make about the Branch Hill, Ohio case that for years may have misled those interested in such matters. The famous drawing of the "trolls under the bridge," with their lopsided chests, was sketched by Stringfield based on his impression of what was seen and was not drawn under the direction of the witness. These froglike "trolls" more properly belong in Fortean creature chronicles than in UFO books, as an incident which took place 17 years later in nearby Loveland makes clear.

In March of 1972, on two separate occasions, two Ohio policemen saw what has become known as the "Loveland Frogman." The incidents were investigated by Ron Schaffner and Richard Mackey, who interviewed the officers.

The first incident took place at 1:00 AM on March 3, 1972 on a clear, cold night. Officer Ray Shockey was on route to Loveland, via Riverside Road, when he thought he saw a dog beside the road, in a field on Twightwee Road. But then the "thing" stood up, its eyes illuminated by the car lights, looked at him for an instant, turned, and leapt over a guardrail. Shockey saw it go down an embankment into the Little Miami River, a mere fifteen or so miles from the Ohio River. He described the thing as weighing about sixty pounds, measuring about three to four feet tall, and having a textured leathery skin and a face like a frog or lizard. Shockey drove to the police station and returned with Officer Mark Matthews to look for evidence of the creature. They turned up scrape marks leading down the side of the small hill near the river.

On St. Patrick's Day, March 17, 1972, Officer Matthews was driving outside of Loveland when he had a similar experience. Seeing an animal lying in the middle of the road, he stopped to remove what he thought was a dead critter. Instead, when the officer opened his squeaky car door, the animal got up into a crouched position like a football player. The creature hobbled to the guardrail and lifted its leg over the fence, keeping an eye on Matthews the whole time.

Perhaps it was the funny smirk on its face, but Matthews decided to shoot it. He missed, however, probably because the thing didn't slow down. Matthews later told how he felt the creature stood more upright than the way Shockey had described it. One area farmer told investigators he saw a large, frog-like or lizard-like creature during the same month of the officers' sightings.

The reports of the 1972 Frogman had been hard on the witnesses. "Those two officers took a lot of flack about the sighting back then," said a local businessman who wished not to be identified in a 1985 newspaper story about the sightings. "People made fun of them and the city."

Years later, in 1999, during interviews, Mark Matthews explained that he was tired of talking about the "Frogman," and that what he had seen was an iguana. But at the time, both witnesses definitely saw something like an upright manlike lizard about 4 feet tall. And then there is the matter of the sketch. Officer Shockey's sister drew it for them shortly after their experience with the creature, and it clearly is a giant frogman, a bipedal creature. During 2001, I asked investigator Ron Schaffner about Matthews' recent attempts to pull back from his original story. Schaffner told me: "Why, after all these years is Matthew's debunking the story? I'm not sure. Could be a number of reasons. But both officers told us that it resembled the sketch in 1976. Why would they shows us a composite drawing of this creature back in 1976 and tell us that it looked like the drawing? I lived in Loveland for about five years and the story is still circulating with many variations. Just maybe Matthews is tired of hearing the story and all the variations."

Those who witnessed similar creatures in 1955 were apparently not available to serve as a safety net for those police officers who saw something in 1972. The ridicule curtain came down hard on them. Can we blame anyone for wishing it never happened to them?

Scrape Ore Lizard Man
A trip to South Carolina in the late 1980s, continues the chronology and our pursuit of the Creatures from the Black Lagoon. And there we find a skeptical law enforcement department.

At 2:00 AM, on June 29, 1988, 17-year-old Christopher Davis was changing a flat tire on his car near Scape Ore Swamp, which is just outside the rural town of Bishopville in South Carolina's Lee County. Davis was placing the car jack into his trunk when he saw something extremely large running on its hind legs toward him from across a field. As it got closer, Davis jumped inside his 1976 Toyota Celica and tried to slam the door shut. Unfortunately for Davis, the thing grabbed the mirror as it attempted to wrench the door open. Davis started the car and floored the gas, but the creature jumped on the car's roof. Luckily, it soon fell off as the vehicle sped away. When Chris arrived home he was trembling with fear, the roof of his car bore a series of long scratches and the wing mirror was severely twisted.

Davis said the creature walked like a human, stood over seven feet tall, had green scaly skin, and red glowing eyes. It had three fingers on each hand and three toes on each foot, each with four-inch long black claws. This nightmarish entity from South Carolina—one of the most bizarre creatures reported in recent times—was aptly nicknamed Lizard Man. As many young people began hanging out in the Scrape Ore Swamp in hopes of seeing it, there were several eyewitness reports that emerged. Teenagers Rodney Nolfe and Shane Stokes, for example, were driving near the swamp with their girlfriends when the Lizard Man darted across the road in front of their car.

Investigating the area around the swamp, State Trooper Mike Hodge and Lee County Deputy Sheriff Wayne Atkinson found three crumbled, forty-gallon cardboard drums. The tops of saplings were ripped off eight feet above the ground. And there were, according to Hodge, "humongous footprints," fourteen-by-seven-inch impressions in hard red clay. Following the tracks for four hundred yards, the officers backtracked and found new prints impressed in their car's tire tracks. According to state wildlife biologists, the footprints matched no known animal species.

On August 18, 1988, Davis passed a private polygraph test. Sumter Police Captain Earl Berry had administered Davis' polygraph at the Sumter City-County Law Enforcement Center.

Lee County Sheriff Liston Truesdale said that another "eyewitness," a Browntown resident, claimed in a sworn statement to have crossed paths with the creature in the fall of 1987; the sheriff's department was first told about this incident in June 1988, before Davis' encounter—but they didn't believe it. They collected the sworn statement on August 13, 1988, after they began to take the Lizard Man seriously. George

Holloman Jr., a 31-year-old construction worker, said he had ridden a bike to a flowing spring about 12:30 AM one day in the fall of 1987. Holloman drank some water, lit a cigarette, turned around and "saw it across the road," Truesdale said.

"What he saw, he thought, was a dead tree that had been struck by lightning. Then it moved." The sheriff said Holloman described it as between seven and eight feet tall, and it "stood up like a man," Truesdale said. "A car passed by, and that's when he saw the eyes. He said they glowed when the car passed." The creature went back in the swamp after the car passed, Holloman told Sheriff Truesdale. "He thought it was a 'haunt,'" what rural folks call ghosts, the sheriff said. Truesdale said Holloman told no one of the encounter. "When he did tell his family, his brother thought he was going fool."

Yet another man, a colonel living in Lee County, reported seeing a "brownish creature about 8 feet tall" on August 26, 1988. Truesdale's office investigated, and the sheriff said he would administer a polygraph test to the man, too. "Everyone who reports seeing something will be given a polygraph test," Truesdale said.

The Lizard Man Mystery

"The trouble in trying to understand all reported monsters," said Charles Fort, "is their mysterious appearances and disappearances."

How true.

Can we really conceptualize that Lizard Beings are real? No wonder people toy with the idea of explaining one mystery with another, that we are seeing visitors that exist on another plane, for example. John Keel believes that Mothman, other glowing-eyed beasties, and Creatures from the Black Lagoon are nothing more than demonological elementals here to cause trouble. In a world gone mad, perhaps he's on to something. With such a wild set of reports, we must think outside the box. What is going on here?

During the 1980s Dale Russell, a Canadian paleontologist, had promoted the idea that reptiles had as much a chance to evolve an intelligent, bipedal form as did the mammals. His drawings of this upright, reptilian, intellectual animal look suspiciously like the composite picture we get from the sightings of the Ohio Valley/Black Lagoon creatures. Are these beasts future time travelers lost in some time/space warp?

Or are they infrequent visitors from an ultraterrestrial plane?

Or have these stepped out of flying saucers?

Or do you feel more comfortable with the idea there is a breeding population of scaly, manlike, upright creatures lingering along the edges of some of America's swamps—cryptids of the upright reptilian variety? Merbeings among us?

Are Lizard Men just contemporary versions of the Mermen, Mermaids, and Merbeings, the water creatures of the past. Fortean author Mark A. Hall certainly feels this may be the case. Perhaps, the mermaids and mermen of ancient lore are still being seen today, he feels, though, apparently, in far lesser numbers. Yet this group of water-connected beings ranges far beyond the merpeople of yore and includes such varieties as the scaly-looking but perhaps misnamed Lizard Men, or the fiery-eyed Latino phenomenon known as the Chupacabras. So perhaps the answer dwells more in the water than on the land.

Something is out there. That's for sure.

CHAPTER 6

The Spawn of Mothman

The sun was just coming up when I left New Orleans, Louisiana, to travel to Honey Island Swamp. The friendly woman driving the mini-van that brings you deeper into the swamp before you use a shallow-bottomed boat said that just the week before Kevin Costner had sat where I was now sitting. I think I was supposed to be happy about the fact that our bottoms had warmed the same cushion. Nevertheless, even though I was struck with the fact that the star of *JFK* and *Waterworld* had traveled the same path I was now taking, I wasn't seeking celebrities. I'd come to hunt a monster, or at least learn more about one – an ogre that left pointed, three-toed prints.

The Honey Island Monster led a quiet life until filmmaker Alan Landsburg and on-camera host Leonard Nimoy featured the creature in their 1970s series "In Search Of." Big, biped and as frightening as any beast you've heard about, sightings of the Honey Island Monster have been drifting out of the bayous for years. When I visited, however, none of the swamp's nature center guides, nor even the woman selling alligator burgers knew anything about the critter. One boatman said he thought that it "sort of looked like Bigfoot." And elements of the creature's fame were in evidence, as I noticed one of the swamp boats was named "Wookie," after the giant hairy Star Wars character.

Thanks to the Honey Island Swamp Tours, my excursion into the bayou was uneventful. There was talk of the monster and I was able to examine its habitat, but you can't expect much else from such tourist-oriented rambles. The New Orleans Zoo had an exhibit of a giant Bigfootlike Honey Island Monster, near their white alligator enclosure. But the Honey Island Monster today lives deeper into the swamps than where these tour boats go. Kevin Costner and I didn't see any monsters, nor many animals, I must admit. Indeed, I was able to get closer to alligators and other wildlife in my canoe trips into the Everglades, Okefenokee, and other southern swamps I have journeyed to alone and with a few associates. That's the way it should be, I suppose. Monsters are for dark nights and campfires, not tourists.

The Honey Island critter left evidence of itself behind, nevertheless. The footprint casts of the creature I had been shown years earlier, indicated that the incorrect name had been given to the swamp boat–the Honey Island Monster is not a Bigfoot. Maybe the footprints are those of alligators, maybe not. In any case, they match what people say the Honey Island Swamp Monsters feet look like.

Today you can even buy copies of these casts online. Local folk author Dana Holyfield sells them along with her small privately bound book entitled *Encounters with the Honey Island Swamp Monster* (1999). In this booklet, she explains that her grandfather, Harlan E. Ford, was the first man to report a sighting of a mysterious creature lurking in Louisiana's Honey Island Swamp. Ford was also the first to get plaster casts of the creature's three and four-toed footprints. "That thing stood eye level with me," said Ford at the time, "and had short dingy gray hair on it's body and long gray hair hung from it's head. The thing that startled me the most, were it's large amber eyes." Harlan Ford and his friends were later interviewed for the documentary series, "In Search Of."

Monsters and More Galore

If recent on-line chatter is any indication, we are entering an era of high interest in reports of unknown hominids and related monsters. However, it all seems to be built on a shallow foundation of understanding for the complex situation that confronts us. E-mail lists and websites appear to be reinforcing the notion that everything huge and hominid, literally around the globe, is only some form of Bigfoot or Sasquatch. Besides being extremely ethnocentric, typically American, and shortsighted, I think it's downright wrong. Such a view completely ignores the diverse spectrum of animals with which we are dealing. Take, for example, one variety—the three-toed, manlike animals (yes, a few researchers like me think there are more than one "type").

The three-toed, perhaps non-reptilian but reptilian-looking "Creatures from the Black Lagoon" are more frequently reported in North America than casual readers of cryptozoology might realize, as we noted in the last chapter. There is a natural screening process that occurs when investigators are challenged by a seemingly bizarre report of a thing that has left behind a print with three sharp prongs. One of the first reactions from field investigators—for example, the professor of biology at the local college—when called upon to make a "positive ID" is disbelief. Their comment usually goes something like: "Well, since all hominids have five digits (or toes) it's obvious that this print must be a fake, a hoax, someone's idea of a joke and a total waste of my time!"

Sadly, Bigfoot is the first frame of reference for news reporters, police officers, zoo keepers, and college professors—often the "first responders" who are called upon when anything big and unknown is seen or an unusual footprint found. That's not to say that things improve when a bona fide Bigfoot hunter shows up.

But let's step back a moment and think about this. If you were going to create a hoax and you wanted to fool your local authorities for even a day or two, would you not put five toes in your fake footprint? After all, most so-called Bigfoot tracks do show five toes. Why would a hoaxer leave such any obviously strange series of prints behind? It defies logic. To suggest that perhaps a different kind of animal, one with three toes, exists in some of America's swamps is just asking too much from some of these folks.

Have I gone too far? As noted at the end of the last chapter, there certainly seems to be a confluence between the large historical body of evidence for real merfolk and the new accounts of these sharp three-toed unknowns. Words escape us. Names fool us. Swamp monsters, goat-suckers, and werewolves. People try to pigeonhole the unclassifiable. Momo, the Missouri Monster, left three-toed prints, as did the Fouke Monster, otherwise known as the featured protagonist of *The Legend of Boggy Creek*. We have to ponder more than the actual plaster casts of the triple-toed Honey Island beasts, and re-examine the witness drawing of 1972's Thetis Lake Monster and the account of the Scape Ore Swamp Lizard Man of 1988. Now, let your eyes drift down to their feet. Read the descriptions below of the Chupacabras and notice its Thetis Lake Monster-like spikes on its body. These are formidable beasts. Scary. Sometimes violent.

The Marvel of the Goatsucker

The single most notable cryptozoological phenomenon of the past decade is undoubtedly the Chupacabras (loosely translated as "Goatsucker") of Hispanic America. The legend of this livestock-slaughtering monster was born in small villages in Puerto Rico in 1995 and quickly spread to Mexico and Hispanic communities in the United States on its way to becoming a worldwide sensation like no unexplained creature since the Bigfoot of the late 1950s and 1960s.

Beginning in March 1995 carcasses of goats, chickens, and other small farm animals, seemingly devoid of blood through a puncture wound, were found near the Puerto Rican towns of Morovis and Orocovis. In September came the first sightings of an animal said to combine the features of a kangaroo, a gargoyle, and the gray alien of abduction lore. It was said to be hairy, about four feet tall, with a large, round head, a lipless mouth, sharp fangs, and huge, lidless red eyes. Its body was small, with thin, clawed, seemingly webbed arms and muscular hind legs. The creature also had a series of pointy spikes running from the top of its head down its backbone. Investigator Jorge Martin drew a widely circulated sketch based on these descriptions and the local media repeated the widely popular name, Chupacabras, in many stories.

Some of these sightings were close encounters that provided detailed observations of the creature. For example, during the second week of August, near Canóvanas, Puerto Rico, at about four in the afternoon, Madelyne Tolentino noticed that the driver of a vehicle pulled up in front of her house appeared frightened. When she approached the large front window to get a better look, she saw a creature walking upright in front of her house with its arms outstretched. It walked in an odd, slow, robotic way, as if land was not its primary habitat. The creature was described as being about four feet tall. Its body appeared to be covered with short fine gray fur with darkened spots, perhaps its pink-purplish skin. Its legs seemed long and skinny and its feet looked like those of a goose with three separate toes. It had long thin arms and hands with three long skinny fingers with claws. A series of protruding "spikes" ran down its spine.

The face of the Chupacabras was striking. It had two little holes for a nose and its mouth was little more than a slash. The creature's eyes protruded, ran up to its temples, and spread to the sides. They looked damp and dark and had no whites to them. It's the sight of those eyes that brought a scream to Tolentino's lips: "My God!" Her mother heard this and went outside to chase the creature, which took off in a hopping motion toward the nearby woods. A boy who works for Tolentino's husband in the machine shop across the street put on gloves and actually managed to grab the creature momentarily. A frightened kid on a bicycle started throwing bottles at the Chupacabras. Later, Tolentino learned that her husband had seen the same creature in the morning, and that evening two church bus drivers also saw it.

Sightings and slain livestock continued to be reported in parts of Puerto Rico throughout the fall of 1995. In March 1996 a segment on the Chupacabras appeared on the TV talk show "Christina," the Spanish-language Univision network's popular counterpart to "Oprah." The media attention from this exposure appears to have caused the migration of Chupamania into Mexico and the United States.

Chupacabras represents folklore in the modern age of electronic telecommunications. Once it took centuries for a legend like the Abominable Snowman to be disseminated through the generations. The stories told now are similar; what has changed is the speed at which the word of mouth travels. They quickly become cross-cultural, just like Jennifer Lopez!

Hispanic television and radio reports ignited the Chupacabras phenomenon, but more significantly, the Chupacabras is the first monster that the Internet can call its own. In 1995, with the World Wide Web explosion occurring, Chupacabras was ideal for the medium. Martin's celebrated Chupacabras sketch was flashed instantly to a global network of anomalist students, online. Meantime, Hispanic-oriented information sources eagerly spread Chupacabras tales. This generated a one-two punch of underground publicity, bridging two cultures, and the Chupacabras phenomenon was in full flower before anyone even knew what it was.

Despite the media and net hysteria, writers and researchers, like North American-based Hispanic cryptozoologist Scott Corrales, gathered and investigated Chupacabras reports in a level-headed fashion. The first major American sighting of the Chupacabras took place in March 1996 in Miami, followed by others in Texas, Arizona, and other North American locations. Alleged Chupacabras' footprints from Florida (which to me look like dog tracks) were sold for $25 each. Chupacabras "sightings" have decreased in frequency since 1996, though the occasional report still surfaces from time to time.

During 2001, Chile appeared to be in a full-scale flap of Chupacabras' reports. A recent example will illustrate this wave, from the files of Jaime Ferrer, director of the Calama UFO Center. From the Chilean city of Calama, on August 28, 2001, at 10:30 PM, a couple, the Martins, were driving back to their home from a church meeting, when they saw a strange figure on the side of the road, on a small hill, coming out of the bushes. The creature seemed to be suspended in the air, a few inches off the ground. The creature was moving very rapidly; in fact, it was too fast for any ordinary animal. The entity rapidly crossed the road in a straight flight pattern. As they watched the strange creature, Mr. Martin and his wife began feeling unusually cold and fearful. "The creature appeared to be very rigid," he said, "with its arms stuck to the body in a very strange way, like defying all laws of physics. It had a ghostly and grotesque aspect. It was gray and white in color and had lots of hair. It almost looked like a hairy coat or a blanket!"

Mr. Martin is a security guard at a local school. He's been married for ten years and lives an ordinary life with his wife and three children. Ferrer's Calama UFO Center looked into the credibility of both witnesses and determined that there is absolutely no reason for them to create a false story. Interestingly, though, Martin reported that as a youth, he once saw a strange bird about three feet tall on his family's cattle ranch. He pointed a flashlight at it. The creature reacted very violently and tore up the wire fence, which is remarkable for any bird. Shades of Mothman.

But in the larger framework of creature accounts, the Chupacabras is, as we shall see, merely the Hispanic version of other things that have been reported elsewhere.

Dover Demon Revisited

Reconsider the Dover Demon, a wonder that occurred a quarter of a century ago in Dover, Massachusetts, USA, when a bright orange beast was seen by locals. I made the initial field investigations and brought in investigators Walt Webb, Joe Nyman, and Ed Fogg to conduct a broad-based, four-person analysis. As Walt Webb, who has since become a well known name in UFO studies, later noted, this was "one of the most baffling creature episodes ever reported."

I was reminded of this creature again by a recent book, *Passing Strange* (Vermont: Chapters Publishing Ltd, 1996), in which Joseph Citro has compiled many elements of the story—as well as by Nevermore Creations 2001-2002 line of action figures, one of which is the Dover Demon. When I coined the name, I could have never guessed this critter would become so famous. In 1977, I assumed that the encounters were unique and would be forgotten the following year. However, the phenomenon appears to be enduring and, I now propose, might have resurfaced across cultural lines far away from the horse barns of Farm Street in Dover. But first a brief summary of the Dover Demon events.

The three separate sightings unfolded quietly in April 1977 in the rural community of Dover, a town with more horses than people. The witnesses described a small, extremely thin, four-foot-tall creature. It had a disproportionately large, figure-of-eight-shaped head and spindly fingers. While there was general agreement on the bright orange color of the hairless body and its sand-paper-textured skin, there was a difference of opinion on the color of its eyes. However, the witnesses were unknown to each other and described essentially the same thing, independently, to all the investigators involved.

Citro does a superb job of chronicling the Dover Demon case through the years. He mentions a second interview with the first and primary witness Bill Bartlett, in 1988, in which Bartlett reaffirmed how frightened he was on the night he saw it. And

Carl Sheridan, the Dover Police Chief whom we all interviewed in 1977, still insists: "It was real."

The Dover-Sherborn High School newspaper, *The Focus*, in October 2000, revisited the Dover Demon reports, too. Student reporter Julie Onufrak tracked down Bill Bartlett who is an artist and still lives in the Boston area. Abby Brabham lives in Vermont and her niece attends Dover-Sherborn. Both were adamant in interviews that they saw something, though they are still not sure what it was.

So what was the Dover Demon? An anomaly? An alien? An elaborate hoax? Mark Hall's little Merbeing? I have some ideas, but I really don't know, of course. What I do feel is that the solution does not exist in the stars. At the time, the theories were many and varied, but the UFO connection was the most popular. I thought it wise to bring in some intelligent ufologists, so it was interesting that, having failed to establish any link with the UFO angle, they eliminated that as a possible answer. UFOs were never a factor in the case and, as I've learned over the years—and as I noted more in depth in my recent revision of *Mysterious America*—using one unknown to explain another is always dangerous.

However, taking a more broad-based view here, perhaps we have always had, at least, precursors and heirs to the Dover Demon right under our noses. Something similar might have happened in Kelly, Kentucky, in 1955. Remember that one? After a vague report of a light in the sky, a group of hairless, silver-skinned, little creatures lay siege to the terrified Sutton family in their farmhouse. Maybe that was just a case screened through a rural American frame of reference and reported in the midst of the "flying saucer" hysteria of the day.

An analogous situation has occurred with the reports of the Chupacabras. Otherworldly origins—both supernatural and alien—are being brought in to explain these perceived creatures but what is happening might have origins much closer to home. Projections show that by the year 2050 the majority population of North America will be Hispanic. Individuals who trace their ancestry to Spain and Portugal, also known as Latinos, are having a prominent impact on American culture, which was once viewed as being mostly Anglo-European with a strong African-American component. Now, the influence of Hispanic cryptozoological trends are being felt across the broad American land-scape. Reflect on this when considering the wide dissemination of things as varied as the Macarena dance craze during the mid-1990s, the popularity of Latin actors and singers, and the panic over the Chupacabras. Ponder on what might be next.

I think we've already had a hint of this influence in places like Brazil and Chile. Take, for instance, what happened in January 1996, when firefighters—who take the place of police in Brazil in responding to crises—farmers and others reported seeing three-to-four-feet tall, bumpy headed, hairless, skinny creatures. The media there have com-pared it to the Chupacabras and claimed that several have been captured and that a coverup backed by the U.S. government is in the works. There was a similar report regarding the creature supposedly captured in Varginha, Brazil in the late 1990s. The point I want to make is that these critters were almost immediately labeled "extraterrestrial," yet, looking at the details, they seem as remote from UFOs as was the Dover Demon.

Small, skinny, hairless creatures might be part of the zoogeography and folklore of the New World. We don't need UFOs to transport them here. From an isolated event in rural Massachusetts to a flap affecting Hispanics throughout the Americas, these things have become part of the fabric of daily life as we live our life in this new century. Do they exist? Sometimes I don't think that's even an important question any-more. They have arrived. Or should I ask, have they merely come into our collective consciousness? They might have been here all along.

Chupacabras of the World

The Chupacabras has raised awareness that all the creatures under the sun may not comfortably exist in the files of cryptozoologists. Nevertheless, a broader view, that the commonality of these things is apparent, from one location to another, is becoming more evident.

Within the tradition of the Dominion Republic, you will find the sightings and tales of the *ciguapas* who swim deep below the blue waters. The Dominican legend of the *ciguapas,* creatures who lived in underwater caves and whose feet were on backward so that humans can't follow their footprints (a motif reported in some Yeti legends), was reinvented in 2000, by author Julia Alvarez, for her children's book, *The Secret Footprints* (Knopf). My contacts in the Dominion Republic, such as Rosa Guzman, daughter of a former prominent government official, and her husband Nick Higgins, have told me that the *ciguapas* may be the island's version of the Chupacabas. People are actively reporting the creature, children pass along tales about it, and local songs, like *La Ciguapas,* are sung islandwide.

Looking to another island, a half a world away, one can see how remarkably alike some of these creatures are. On Madagascar, the native peoples, the Sakalava and Bara, talk of their *kalanoro*. All the tribes of Madagascar believe in them, according to Raymond Decary, who researched the common themes connecting the stories of the *kalanoro* back in the 1950s. Some tribes see the *kalanoro* as amphibious creatures. Around Lake Aloatra, they are thought to be females who live at the bottom of the water and are said to have hair that falls to their waist, like naiads or mermaids.

But around Lake Kinkony, the Sakalava tribe regards the *kalanoro* as males who live in the thickets and reeds on the edges of lagoons. They are said to be less than three feet high, have sweet female voices, and possess but three toes on each foot. They supposedly live on fish and raw food, and lead humans astray.

Other tribes, however, regard the *kalanoro* as a land dweller. The Betsileo tribe, for instance, thinks the *kalanoro* is a little female land dwarf, not more than two feet high and covered with hair. In northern Madagascar the *kalanoro* are thought to live in woods and caves and have hooked nails that inflict cruel wounds on all who try to capture them. And to the Bara tribe, the *kalanoro* are quick and nimble little forest dwellers with long hair, who reside in the Ankazoabo district and come out at night to search the villages for food.

How recent are the encounters with the *kalanoro*? The most up-to-date reports come from professor Joe Hobbs of the University of Missouri-Columbia's Department of Geography, who studied in the Ankarana Special Reserve, Madagascar, during the late 1990s. On May 15, 2000, when Hobbs wrote his report, he talked of how "the people of the nearby village of Ambalakedi consider Andoboara Cave sacred because on three separate occasions, most recently just two years previously, grief-stricken parents whose children had wandered into the forest had recovered them alive here. The children had been abducted by a sometimes malevolent spirit called *kalanoro* who sought to rebuke the parents for not taking proper care of their children. The parents sought guidance from another spirit called *tromba* who possessed a fellow villager and recited a laundry list of demands made by the *kalanoro,* which would have to be met for the children to be found. Once the parents fulfilled their obligations by, for example, leaving honey and sacrificing zebu cattle in the place designated by the *tromba*, the *kalanoro* revealed via the *tromba* the lost children's location—in each case, the joyous reunion took place in the Andoboara Cave. As I was to learn in the coming weeks, there are countless caves in Madagascar bearing rich accounts of this kind."

These "legends may be fantastic," wrote French zoologist Bernard Heuvelmans in 1955, but "they are found all over Madagascar, and it would be odd if they were utterly without foundation," especially given the fact that "some areas of Madagascar are still almost unexplored, such as the Ambongo reserve and the lonely Isalo mountains, and there are still some 3 or 4 million hectares of virgin forest...." These reports of the amphibious, three-toed *kalanoro*, of course, match remarkably well other reports of Chupacabras, Creatures from the Black Lagoon, and other Merbeings from around the world.

Shape-shifters and Demoniacs

Other creatures have been given more sinister labels. Long before the name Bigfoot became attached to most North American reports of strange, upright, hairy creatures, people were seeing things that were bipedal and furry. But what were eyewitnesses calling them? Apeman? Gorilla? Wildmen? Yes, all of those and even Sasquatch in western Canada since the 1920s. But what about werewolf?

Needless to say, the term "werewolf" has been applied to several unique beasts down through the years, especially in certain parts of North America. A belief in *lycanthropy* is a well-known, living tradition in both Louisiana and Quebec. Native Americans, especially in the American

Southwest, thought of werewolves as real animals. The *loup-garou* (French for werewolf), as they were called in Canada, were described by Nancy Garden in her book *Werewolves* (Philadelphia: Lippincott, 1973) as "certain kind of Canadian werewolf, like the Navajo variety...said to dig up graves." (Hold that mental image in your head.)

But what of the English-speaking sections of the American continent? Hunting down such accounts, mining them from the huge number of possible sources, is often a bibliographical and cryptozoological nightmare. But in the U.S., at least, this task is being made easier daily by an explosion of little "local color" books and booklets, especially those that tune in to an area's true-life *X-Files* stories. Small, regional books like these, often self-published, are an excellent source for these little-known stories.

One such book, *The W-Files: True Reports of Wisconsin's Unexplained Phenomena* by Jay Rath (Madison: Wisconsin Trails, 1997), contains a newly-revealed old report that deserves our attention. One night in 1936, just east of Highway 18, near Jefferson, Wisconsin, Mark Schackelman encountered a bizarre beast that was digging in an old Indian burial mound. (Remember that Navajo legend?) It was covered in black hair, stood more than six feet tall, and had an odor like decaying meat. One of the strangest things about it was that it had a shriveled thumb and forefinger, giving it a three-fingered appearance. Its muzzle looked like something between an ape and a dog, which, along with its pointed ears, gave it a very unique classic werewolf look.

The next night, Schackelman returned to the ancient mound and saw the creature again. This time, the thing seemed to be making some distinctive vocalizations, almost "neo-human," he would call them. Mark's son, Joe Schackelman, editor and publisher of the *Kenosha Labor* newspaper, later wrote up his father's sighting: "My father's first thought was that it must be something satanic, so immediately he prayed, and he said it seemed to show some fear at that." As the elder Schackelman and the creature carefully and steadily backed away from each other, the thing "made a three-syllable growling noise that sounded like '*gadara*,' with the emphasis on the second syllable." Then it disappeared.

As Biblical scholar Daryl R. Coats has pointed out, Gadara is the name of a place in Israel, with the countryside surrounding Gadara known as "the country of the Gadarenes." Furthermore, Coats notes, in Mark 5 (cf. Matt. 8), two "demoniacs" lived in Gadara—demoniacs who "met him [Jesus] out of the tombs" and who "had [their] dwelling among the tombs" (something suspiciously similar to digging in an Indian grave site) and whose "unclean spirit[s]" feared God (v. 7) and left when commanded to do so. The message from this Wisconsin were-wolf, as heard by Schackelman, may then have a spiritual context, thanks to these insights from Coats. The demons of Gadara are a very real part of Judeo-Christian tradition, and praying was an appropriate thing for the witness to do.

Bizarrely, this utterance is also very close to the sound of the name of a similar beast reported in the Orient and India—the Gadura. John Keel pointed out when he was investigating the Mothman sightings that the Garuda reminded him of the entity he was tracking. Indeed, Keel subtitled the original version of *The Mothman Prophecies*, thusly: *An Investigation into the Mysterious American Visits of the Infamous Feathery Garuda.*

This 1936 sighting occurred about two miles from a July 1964 sighting of a big hairy "thing," seven-to-eight-feet tall, which ran in front of TV technician Dennis Fewless' car before jumping a five-foot barbed wire fence. Again, on November 30, 1968, in the Deltox Marsh near Fremont, Wisconsin, twelve hunters saw a short, dark brown-haired, hairless-faced beast that left three-toed, webbed tracks in the snow as it passed in front of them. They were afraid to shoot at it because it looked too human-like.

Reports of supposed werewolves are common in southern Wisconsin, as newspeople attempt to give a name and focus to accounts that lie outside the familiar realm of the Bigfoot reports. Linda Godfrey, a reporter for *The Week* of Walworth County, has collected local "were-wolf" stories from her area for 40 years and appeared on the reality tele-vision program "Inside Edition" discussing them.

The broader context of these reports embrace sightings of the triple-toed Honey Island Swamp Monster, the three-fingered and three-toed Thetis Lake Monster, and the similarly-digited Scape Ore Swamp Lizard

Man. The Gadara demoniac and the Dover Demon appear to be kin and the observation by remarkably close eyewitnesses sheds some light on whether these beasts have the same three or five digits on their hands and feet. Indeed, the Gadara creature's shriveled thumb and forefinger would certainly give it a three-fingered appearance.

"Ufology is just another name for demonology," John Keel told me, a week before the September 11th attack on the World Trade Center, which occurred just a couple of miles from where he lives.

CHAPTER 7

Keel's Children

*There is not wanting a feast of broad, joyous
humor, in this stranger phantasmagoria, where
pit and stage, and man and animal, and earth
and air, are jumbled in confusion worse
confounded.*—THOMAS CARLYLE

It was a gathering the likes of which occurs all too rarely among investigators. The occasion was the 69th birthday of John A. Keel, the classic writer on the unexplained whom I consider a friend. A small group
of cryptozoologists, Forteans, and ufologists gathered at a little eating
place, the Delphi, in New York City, to celebrate Keel's natal milestone.
Attendees included another friend, Patrick Huyghe, co-editor of The
Anomalist, skeptic George Hansen, Jungian scholar Dennis Stillings,
ventriloquist Doug Skinner, ufologist Antonio Huneeus, parapsycholo-
gist Alexander Imich, and others.

Here I was in New York City, sitting with the man who is most connected with Mothman, listening to his sharp tongue and wit. The defini-
tive book about the Mothman flap is, of course, Keel's *The Mothman
Prophecies*, a work that is equal parts journalism and melodramatic nonfiction, and based on Keel's own unique style of investigation and interviews with eyewitnesses. It is not the kind of book you can read when
alone in your home at night. Keel ties in the Mothman appearances with
UFO sightings that were also reported in and around Point Pleasant,
weaving a bizarre tapestry of extra- and ultraterrestrials, elementals,
tricksters, Men In Black, the CIA, and a huge conspiracy of silence.

Something real was there for Keel to report on, and his influence has been great. We do know that in 1966 and 1967, large birdlike creatures were seen near Point Pleasant. Keel's later writings tended to lump together all of the reports of large, man-sized, gray-bodied, glowing red-eyed creatures in his special way of chronicling the events in the context of other weirdness. Although the cases may perhaps have been identified as something entirely mundane, Keel's work led some to speculate in other directions, such as whether the creatures were aliens, robotic devices, or other elementals, entities on another plane.

Keel has had an impact far beyond what even he could have imagined. As Keel recently said to me, "don't trust cult literature," knowing of course the joke in this advice is that John's work has fostered an incredible, almost cultlike following in his wake. So who is John A. Keel and what do people see in his works that is so captivating? Why has his articles and books had such a profound effect on so many?

John A. Keel

John A. (for Alva) Keel was born on March 25, 1930, in Hornell, New York (although he grew up in nearby Perry) with the given name Alva John Kiehle. As a teenager, in 1944, he began his long writing career, editing a local newspaper column. The detailed works of anomalist Charles Fort (1874-1932) inspired Keel. Another early influence was the stories of Richard S. Shaver, found in the science fiction pulp magazine, *Amazing Stories*. Shaver's tales, said to be true, and promoted by early *Fate* magazine editor Ray Palmer, told of cave and underground entities, the teros and deros.

In 1946 Keel moved to Greenwich Village and began to surround himself with poets, painters, psychics, and publishers, most of who were Forteans, in New York City. By 1952, he was producing a radio program heard by millions called "Things In The Sky" about unidentified flying objects. Through most of the 1950s and early 1960s, Keel lived as a radio and television screenwriter. Keel is private about some details of his life.

"In the Army I studied psychological warfare," Keel told *Steamshovel Press* editor Kenn Thomas during a 1993 interview. "I was a propaganda writer in the Army. I know quite a bit about psychology."

In *Jadoo*, Keel's 1957 autobiography (he would have been 27 when this was published), he tells of searching for the Yeti in the Himalayas. In 1966 he wrote a humorous book called *The Fickle Finger of Fate.*

Then in the mid-1960s, he received a good advance on a UFO book that was supposed to be groundbreaking in its theories. This gave Keel the freedom to spend much time in the field, traveling to the sites of several major incidents. In some cases, such as Point Pleasant in 1966-1967, Keel acted almost like an anthropologist, getting to know the local people and gaining their trust. Through these contacts, Keel became a lightning rod for reports and was able to gather many accounts that would have been unavailable to a more conventional journalist. His gentle personal style was endearing and people were delighted to share their stories with him. Keel "covered the UFO beat as no other during the sixties," notes Patrick Huyghe in *Swamp Gas Times.*

Keel became a friend, generous correspondent, and fellow researcher to many. For example, I met him through my friend Ivan T. Sanderson, and Keel then introduced me to Jerome Clark in 1969. Keel was a buddy of James Moseley, Gary Barker, Norman Mailer, and other Fortean or Greenwich Village-based early writers.

Keel produced many articles for the men's magazines, such as *Saga, True,* and *Mate,* as well as wrote several seminal books, including *UFOs: Operation Trojan Horse* (1970), *Our Haunted Planet* (1971), *The Mothman Prophecies* (1975), and *The Eighth Tower* (1975). Trips to some forty countries and many states led to more articles for *Playboy, Fate,* and *Flying Saucer Review,* some of which appear in compilations like *Disneyland of the Gods: Somebody is Watching You!* (1995). Though Keel has authored 30 books, most are actually *not* about UFOs. Today he continues to write a bimonthly column for *Fate* called "Beyond the Known."

And, of course, there are all the books that got away. John Keel once wrote a book that will never be published. In the 1980s, Keel got a contract for an opus on unidentified submerged objects (USOs), mystery objects that people would report from the world's oceans. Keel worked hard, did a good deal of research on the subject, analyzed all the reports coming out of Scandinavian waters mostly, and began writing. But his intended publisher eventually lost the manuscript in the back of a taxi.

But the real Keel may forever remain a mystery. He told me on

October 9, 2001 that astronomer J. Allen Hynek, who was UFO consultant to the Air Force's Project Blue Book, "was paid to distribute a totally fake bio of me in 1967, and it is still circulating, though everyone in the leper colony keeps adding more crap to it. Be very, very wary."

Keel's following has grown, in large part, because of his crusty and exciting style of writing. Colin Wilson once remarked that Keel was "incapable of writing a dull sentence." Skeptic and librarian Bill Wines (2001) throws the sort of typical praise one reads on the internet about Keel's books: "The best space-goblin book I've ever read is John Keel's *Mothman Prophecies*. If someday there are scholars who specialize in 20th-century saucer literature, they will undoubtedly regard *Mothman* as the nonpareil classic of its genre....Keel was the first prominent UFO researcher, I believe, to propose that the phenomenon was not simply malevolent, but malevolent in a peculiarly mischievous fashion—sick practical jokers in the fashion of the 'little people' of Eire. This view was cleverly summed up in the title of another of Keel's books, *Disneyland of the Gods*. Earth, and its inhabitants, represents a sort of vast theme park for intelligences bent on entertaining themselves at our expense....Keel was convinced that the space goblins were extra-dimensional creatures that could manipulate matter and energy at will, send messages telepathically, and read minds. He chronicled their activities in gripping, paranoia-laced prose that became his trademark."

But it wasn't always that way. During the years of his Mothman pursuits, Keel's approach to his topics changed. "I abandoned the extraterrestrial hypothesis in 1967," he wrote in *Operation Trojan Horse*, "when my own field investigations disclosed an astonishing overlap between psychic phenomena and UFOs....I feel that the ultimate solution [to the UFO question] will involve a complicated system of new physics related to theories of the space-time continuum....The objects and apparitions do not necessarily originate on another planet and may not even exist as permanent constructions of matter. It is more likely that we see what we want to see and interpret such visions according to our contemporary beliefs."

Meanwhile, more conventional or old-school ufologists have felt that Keel has no place in the UFO field. Jerome Clark has noted that

Keel's speculations placed him closer to being an occultist, and has written that Keel is "nothing so much as a demonologist." Clark goes on: "Whereas traditional ufologists took a relatively conservative approach, seeking testimony from trained observers and putting a premium on radar/visual and multiply-witnessed sightings, and viewed exotic claims with suspicion, Keel vigorously championed everything from Mothman to contactees. Many ufologists doubted that the former—a monstrous birdlike entity reported over a several month period by persons living along the Ohio River—had anything to do with UFOs, and they had long ranked the latter (individuals who claimed ongoing communications with friendly extraterrestrials) among the crooked and the crazy. Keel, however, argued that 'ultraterrestrials'—supernatural 'transmogrifications' of paranormal energy from an unimaginable other reality—have been pestering, frightening, manipulating, and even destroying human beings from the beginning of mankind's history."

John Keel's generally radical approach to ufology has placed him outside the mainstream of the field. But as the decades pass, many young people interested in UFOs and such have grown to accept his conclusions more and more, in spite of his own wishes to the contrary.

With the release of the documentaries *Secrets of the Shadow World* (George Kuchar, 2000) and *Search for the Mothman* (David Grabias, 2002), and the motion picture *The Mothman Prophecies* (Mark Pellington, 2002), John A. Keel and his work will be exposed to a whole new audience. Some will become followers.

Banshees

A strong sense of the foreboding dread of gloom underlies our sense of Mothman, and Keel's chronicling of all the events leading up to the collapse of the Silver Bridge certainly has helped that feeling along. The chilling conclusion of *The Mothman Prophecies,* after months of sightings of a glowing, red-eyed giant creature of the darkness, seems archetypical and familiar. I call it "Keelian." Perhaps this is so because the tradition of the banshee exists in the background of Keel's special brand of story telling. Or even the foreground? In his *Strange Creatures of Time and Space,* Keel writes about the ghostly creatures he chases, noting: "They scream like banshees (maybe they are the original banshees of folklore)." This phantasmagoria has become Keel's children, banshees all.

In Irish and Scottish experiences (please note I use this word purposely as I speak here of more than legends), rural peoples would tell of screaming entities coming to visit before a death, a sign of a life's end being close at hand. The banshee, a female fairy that would wail before a death, is often very closely tied to a specific lineage.

On her Celtic-Connection.com website, Cynthia Austin has written in "The Banshee–The Celtic Death Messenger": "The Gaelic terms used most frequently to describe the banshee are the 'bean-si' (a female dweller of a sidhe, or fairy mound), the 'bean chaointe' (a female keener, a term found in east Munster and Connaught) and the 'badhb' (referring to a more dangerous, frightening bogey). Although 'bean-si' implies an Otherworld or fairy being, the banshee is a solitary creature without male counterpart who never partakes in communal human or fairie social enterprise. Speculation also links the banshee with the mystical race Tuatha De'Dannan, from whence the fairy folk are descended. There is little folk evidence to support Christian explanations that the banshee is a devil who wails for the souls that are lost to her as they ascend to heaven…the banshee should be thought of as the 'spirit of the family,' a spirit who attends to the family in a time of transition."

As Jerome Clark and I were writing *Creatures of the Outer Edge*, Clark, who today is known more for his encyclopedic ufological books, told me of his family's personal banshee. His great-great grandmother resided in rural Ireland until the mid-nineteenth century, where she and her family lived in terror of the "Black Fairy." The entity's appearance inevitably presaged a death in the family. It came, family members were told, apparently, to take the dead one's soul away. In recent discussions with Clark, the family had mostly forgotten about its memory of this legacy, and I had to remind him of our talks about this some 25 years earlier. Even today, it appears, people are allowing family traditions of the banshee to pass into unrecovered recollections. That is until another sudden appearance of the red-eyed pooka presents itself.

Hounds from Hell

John Keel's view of Mothman and its kin have called forth a whole reex-amination of many critters, down through the years. One Keel likes especially was the red-eyed, huge black dogs. They are an easy transition from red-eyed winged weirdies, and examples of some very strange encounters literally jump out at us.

Take, for instance, this bizarre little episode, cited by David Webb (the ufologist brother of Dover Demon investigator Walter Webb) in Webb's *1973: Year of the Humanoids*:

> September 9, Savannah, Georgia: "Ten big, black hairy
> dogs" emerged from a landed UFO in Laurel Grove
> Cemetery and ran through the cemetery. The UFO turned
> out its lights after landing. Several youths made the report.

To read an account like this and conclude that black dogs are "UFO occupants" is to miss the point. The overwhelming majority of black dog stories do not involve anything remotely similar to UFOs. But such reports do suggest something about the "reality" inhabited by UFOs and black dogs and poltergeists and phantom cats. This is Keel's reality, and it is the "reality" of nightmares, which constantly reshuffle the contents of the unconscious mind and manufacture ever-changing syntheses of those contents, with all manner of seemingly unrelated ideas and images coming together briefly, then splitting apart, then merging again in other, even stranger forms. The motifs of fairylore and UFO phenomenology therefore become so hopelessly entwined in the wake of some cases that the investigator cannot tell whether he is dealing with reports of "elves" or of "extraterrestrials." If he decides one way or another, he arbitrarily isolates the event—"freezes" it, in other words, when in fact it is fluid.

Confronted with incidents of this type, proponents of the theory of extraterrestrial UFOs invariably speculate that the creatures are "test ani-mals"—an astoundingly anthropomorphic notion if there ever was one. Keel would have none of this, and spawned a wide of range of followers on both sides of the ocean. Some agreed with these Keelian ideas, includ-ing John Rimmer who would write in the *Merseyside UFO Bulletin*,

(December 1970): "As ufologists we seem prepared to accept that such matters as UFO propulsion methods, alien physiology, and advanced technologies may be so far advanced beyond anything we are able to comprehend that they will appear to us as 'magic.' Yet, paradoxically, we also seem prepared to assume that the beings behind such marvels are going to behave exactly like us when we meet them face to face."

Actually "black dogs" are nothing new to our terrestrial environment, as students of folklore and demonology will readily attest. Known widely in many cultural traditions; these seemingly supernatural beasts are considered demonic creatures and are sometimes called "the hounds of hell." Conan Doyle got the inspiration for his classic *The Hound of the Baskervilles* from just such legends. As with the Irish Pooka, these huge black ghost-like dogs have eyes of fire. Going further, Janet and Colin Bord in *Alien Animals* (1981) link Black Shuck and other Celtic black dog traditions to ufological activity.

We have here modern reports of a supernatural entity well known to students of folklore: the black dog, which is apparently a prototype of some of today's more phantomlike, red-eyed black panthers. The black dog, however, is more clearly paranormal, if I may be allowed to use this word briefly here: it has never been mistaken—for very long, at any rate—for a conventional zoological phenomenon or cryptid. The black dog figures prominently in the literature of witchcraft, in which Satan takes the form of a dark hellhound with glowing eyes. Their appearance is often associated with death. Thus it is fitting that in the present instance the witness observes them in a graveyard, just as the last chapter's werewolf-like *Gadara*. To see them is to know that one is "damned," another sinister form of the banshee motif.

The most frightening of the early accounts is preserved in a report prepared by one Abraham Fleming, who claimed not to be repeating a folk tale but to be recording something he himself had witnessed—an event, he conceded, "which to some will seem absurd."

The incident supposedly occurred on Sunday, August 4, 1577, at Bongay, a town ten miles from Norwich, during a violent storm. Inside the local church the congregation sat in almost total darkness, the only light coming from frequent "fearful flashes of lightning." Then, a giant black dog appeared, and ran between two people who were kneeling if in prayer. The dog "wrung the necks of them both at one instant," and they died. At a nearby town, Blibery, seven miles away, on the same day, a black dog "in the same shape and similitude" killed two others. This black dog or one like it was seen thereabouts by others of the church, and terrified people for some time.

The following story, which Sidney Benton of Homcastle, Lincolnshire, related to British Fortean Nigel Watson, is another:

It was during the winter months of 1922 and 1923, when I was employed at a small local dairy, my job was to fetch up the cows from the fields, help to milk them and then deliver it to local people.

Part of my deliveries took me to one of the oldest parts of town—usually took a short cut by going past an old Iron Foundry, over a small bridge with a water-wheel near it, then by the back of the Vicarage and past-the old church- yard. On this particular evening I had made my deliveries and had just climbed over the small wooden palings on my way back to the dairy, when all at once, right in the center of the path, appeared two great bright shining eyes.

I called out, thinking the dog from the dairy, had followed me, but got no answer. I climbed back over the fence and stood there almost petrified with fear. I don't know how long I stood there but suddenly the eyes were just blotted out. I must have been braver then than I am now, for I took my courage in both hands and got back over the fence and walked back over to the spot where the eyes had been.

My employer and his wife and niece, noting that I looked white and frightened, asked the reason. They informed me that the dog had not left the dairy. After this experience, I was always sent on this particular part of my deliveries in daylight. On mentioning my experience to an old lady neighbor, she said that the spot was reputed to be haunted, as some people had been drowned when the ice gave way on the moat of what used to be an old castle there. workmate friend tells me that he had seen the same thing years earlier.

It was such a long time ago, but all I can, remember of that night are the eyes appearing quite suddenly, only a few yards in front of me, at about two or three feet from the ground. I do remember that everything was still and quiet and that after what seemed quite a few minutes the eyes were just blotted out. I have always been convinced that this was something very strange, and the attitude of my employers at the time strengthened my belief. They did not wish to talk about it, and would never let me go that way at night afterwards; and also someone would accompany me when I had to take the pony to the field at nights.

The following incident took place during World War II and was reported in a letter to writer Janet Bord:

The cottage where we lived is still in existence, in Bredon, Worcestershire. My encounter took place one late afternoon in summer, when I had been sent to bed, but was far from sleepy. I was sitting at the end of the big brass bedstead, playing with the ornamental knobs [the witness was a young girl], and looking out of the window, when I was aware of a scratching noise, and an enormous black dog had walked from the direction of the fireplace to my left. It passed round the end of the bed, between me and the window, round the other corner of the bed, towards the door. As the dog passed between me and the window, it swung its head round to stare at me—it had very large, very red eyes, which glowed from inside as if lit up, and as it looked at me I was quite terrified, and very much aware of the creature's breath, which was warm and strong as a gust of wind. The animal must have been very tall, as I was sitting on the old-fashioned bedstead, which was quite high, and our eyes were level. Funnily enough, by the time it reached the door, it had vanished: I assure you that I was wide awake at the time, and sat for quite some long while wondering about what I had seen, and to be truthful, too scared to get into bed, under the covers, and go to sleep. I clearly remember my mother and our host, sitting in the garden in the late sun, talking, and hearing the ringing of the bell on the weekly fried-fish van from Birmingham, as it went through the village! I am sure I was not dreaming, and have never forgotten the experience, remembering to the last detail how I felt, [and] what the dog looked like.

Black dogs are not solely a British phenomenon, of course. Stories of their appearances can be found in American folklore texts and folksongs. Often these incidents are reported not as popular yarns, but as actual experiences of the informants. Theodore Ebert of Pottsville, Pennsylvania, gave this fairly typical account to George Korson, who printed it in his book, *Black Rock: Mining Folklore of the Pennsylvania Dutch*:

One-night when I was a boy walking with friends along Seven Stars Road, a big black dog appeared from nowhere and came between me and one of my pals. And I went to pet the dog but it disappeared right from under me. I couldn't see where it got to. Just like the snap of a finger it disappeared. Well, 1'll tell you, I had about two miles to go to get home, and I made it in nothing flat. I [had] never seen anything like that and I never hope to see anything like it again. This happened later to others. No one in the locality had a dog of that type and it was seen by others with practically the same experience.

No one could ever explain why or where it came from."

The years following World War II brought UFOs into the black dog picture. There is the Savannah, Georgia, report of ten black dogs running from a landed UFO, mentioned earlier. There is also a 1963 story from South Africa. Two men driving at night on the Potchefstroom/

Vereeniging road were startled to see a strange, large, doglike animal cross the road in front of them. Curious, they stopped, only to have a UFO buzz their car several times, frightening them severely and driving all thoughts of the peculiar animal out of their heads.

The following fascinating account was passed along, through a letter from Betty Hill, herself a percipient in a famous and much-publicized UFO case:

In the spring of 1966, Eliot, Maine, was the scene of unusual UFO activity. They came up the river in [the] early evening in groups, night after night. Since this river runs by the flight line at Pease AF Base, they had numerous planes flying, as well as helicopters, and private planes. So it was a spectacular sight—with the sky full of UFOs and flying craft. People came for miles—traffic was bumper to bumper. Police called in police from other areas to direct traffic. People had telescopes, cameras, binoculars. Someone had set up a huge searchlight in a field. Pushcarts sold hot dogs, hamburgers, snacks, cold and hot drinks. In the two to three months that this activity covered, many strange things happened.

One night a group of prominent people from Portsmouth [New Hampshire] decided to go to Eliot to watch the UFOs. After driving around in a caravan of three or four cars, in all the traffic, they decided to pullover in a gravel pit and watch the skies. They all got out when they saw a huge dark "dog" run through the pit. This dog was larger than any they knew so they decided to try to follow it. They ran through the pit, but unfortunately for the last one in the line, he was stopped by a strange odor. He tried to identify it, and as he was standing there, suddenly a form glided towards him. The form was giving off this odor and he had the feeling he was to follow this gliding form. He broke away and ran back to the car, and told a person who remained behind what had happened. She got out of the car and called for the others to return to the car. Fortunately they did, for at this moment, the first man jumped out of the car, saying that he had to go back, and started for the woods. The others grabbed him and held him until he quieted down, and then they all left the area, promising not to reveal what had happened.

From western Pennsylvania, Stan Gordon, the leading investigator of such occurrences, wrote about the following encounter in the *MUFON 1974 UFO Symposium Proceedings*:

Besides the reports of large hairy bipeds being observed, there were sightings of animals about as large as a German Shepherd dog. These animals baffled the witnesses because they couldn't figure out just what kind of animal they were looking at. The creature looked like a cross between a monkey and a dog. It had a tail with rings around it and large red eyes. These creatures at times came up on people's porches and were scared away by the occupants of the house. The witnesses normally were attracted to the creature by the sound of a crying baby, which they speculated that someone had dropped off. When they went to the porch, they found the creature making the sound.

On October 25, 1969, the occupants of a car driving down Exeter Road in Okehampton, Devonshire, England, saw a "Great Dane" appear in front of them. Before they could stop, they had driven right through the "animal," which then disappeared.

At dawn one day late in April 1972 Coastguard Graham Grant at watch over the harbor entrance to the beach at Great Yarmouth, Norfolk, England, noticed something out of the ordinary. "It was," he told the *London Evening News* for April 27, 1972, "a large, black hound-type dog on the beach. It was about a quarter of a mile away from me. What made me watch it was that it was running, then stopping, as if looking for someone. As I watched, it vanished before my eyes. I kept on looking for a time but it did not reappear." Because bulldozers had recently leveled the beach, there was no place the dog could have disappeared. Two years later, in April and May 1974, residents of Hampshire and Cheshire reported a mysterious doglike animal. Some said it was "half cat, half dog."

Huge black dogs have been reported within the so-called Bridgewater Triangle, in the Hockomock Swamp, in Massachusetts. In 1976, I investigated sightings of a huge black "killer dog" reported in Abington which is within this very Keelian window area. The "dog" ripped out the throats of two ponies. Local firefighter Phillip Kane, the owner of the ponies, saw the "dog" standing over the bloody carcasses gnawing at their necks. He said that the "dog" eluded extensive police searches and, for a period of several weeks, terrorized the community. During the three days following the killing of the ponies, police received a thousand telephone calls. School children were kept in at recess, and many homeowners and storekeepers armed themselves with rifles. In other words, it was a full-scale flap taking place. The last time this "dog" was seen was when police officer Frank Curran sighted it along some railroad tracks. The officer fired a shot but "missed." The "black dog" merely turned away and walked off slowly in the other direction.

Since the time of Keel's greatest influence, the 1970s, other works that have touched on this subject, via Fortean insights, for example the Bords in *Alien Animals* (1985) or Jerome Clark's *The Unexplained!* (1992), Patrick Harpur's *Daimonic Reality* (1995), or via fiction like *Black Dogs* (1992) by Ian McEwan. These black dogs are not about cryptozoology, but belong in the folkloric literature. Keel understood where these hounds resided. Speaking of what Keel liked to call "demon dogs," he casually notes in *Strange Creatures* that "spectral dogs have always held a prominent place in occult lore....

"Something wicked this way comes...."

Bray Road Beast
Borderland phenomena do not recognize boundaries.

"The werewolf," John Keel writes, "can presumably pop up any-where."

Wisconsin researcher Richard Hendricks summarizes what many have found: "We note that Keel believes most creatures seen by witnesses are paranormal."

In 1991, near the 1936 sightings of the werewolf Gadara, local buzz, sightings, and accounts began circulating of the Beast of Bray Road. Linda Godfrey, a former Wisconsin news reporter, began collecting what she could find on the critter. In her first article on the early cases, which appeared in *The Week* on December 29, 1991, Godfrey wrote: "The rumors floated around town for two years or so before I heard them. A wolfish-looking creature that ran on two legs had been seen around the Bray Road area, stealing chickens, eating roadkills, and scaring the day-lights out of locals who (sometimes literally) ran into it. A certain num-ber of people, good honest working folk, had seen something—some-thing unusual. Something scary. Something hairy that relished pavement patty dinners! The logical place to start was with the county Humane Officer, Jon Fredrickson. It turned out Fredrickson has a manila folder in his files marked 'Werewolf,' filled with notecards detailing six or seven such 'sightings.' One referred to unusual tracks, another to a hairy pointy-eared creature seen chasing down a deer on two legs."

Throughout 1992 and 1993, a local flap of encounters was in full swing. The media circus had come to town. State Representative Chuck Coleman (no relation) declared he was a candidate for Congress, and said he had been endorsed by the "werewolf." Things got crazy in Wisconsin. Indeed, Coleman dressed up as a "wolfman" for publicity photographs.

On August 13, 1999, a local woman reported she saw the Beast and described it as having "glowing eyes," which Wisconsin Fortean Richard Hendricks noted is the first time that such a detail had ever been mentioned.

The Bray Road Beast, of course, is rooted in the Wisconsin legacy of the 1936 Gadara, a creature tied to the Keelian way of viewing the world, I suspect, because it is a beast beyond the parameters of understanding.

Thinking about the early Gadara case and the related stories of the Bray Road Beast, Hendricks wrote:

One of our favorite Fortean writers is John A. Keel. We like him because he's an idea man. Sometimes the stranger the idea, the better. Keel's an experienced investigator, having talked to thousands of witnesses while getting involved in some of the most famous paranormal events of the 20th Century, from the Mothman sightings to the Hopkinsville Siege of 1955. He's written a string of books, each seemingly weirder than the previous, filled with dark imaginings, paranoia, and the flat out bizarre....

Keel posits that different paranormal beings seen throughout time are really manifestations from the same source. These entities appear to us in accordance with different belief systems. To some, these figures are trickster figures; to others, devils, to others, fairies or aliens or leprechauns. Or gods. Or robots or Men In Black or many other multifarious and sometimes malignant manifestations. They are legion, literally. He calls them Ultraterrestrials.

Ultraterrestrials are beings from the superspectrum, from dimensions or frequencies or energy levels beyond what we can perceive with our limited human perceptions. They exist beyond the three dimensions with which we are familiar. These entities have the ability to cruise up and down the spectrum, to change their very vibration or wave frequencies, and become manifest to our human senses. As they move through the spectrum, they suddenly materialize into the visible spectrum, and thus we see them. As they continue moving through, they dematerialize out of our spectrum, and we no longer see them. Able to control their frequency, they seemingly wink into existence, or out. Along with their ability to change energy or frequency, they have the ability to take whatever form or appearance they desire.

We have no way of testing this theory. But it's wonky, dances to a good beat, and we are sometimes persuaded of its ability to explain certain repetitious phenomena. However, as occasionally persuasive as this theory is, there is no method of testing the validity of the existence of Ultraterrestrials, and so we cannot fully endorse it, as it's unprovable.

Make of that what you will, we but find some interesting parallels between Keel's theories and certain aspects of the Beast story. Theory aside, Keel has documented many instances of these beings appearing in any number of tricked out disguises, offering cryptic bits of conversation to the people who see them. These beings sometimes speak, saying "We are One" or "We are in Bondage." Keel claims this may be an acknowledgment to us of our basic oneness with the superspectrum, that all of us are linked together through subtle waves of energy.

The superspectrum sometimes may be equated with Divine Energy. Keel points out that many of us long for or invite total unity with the superspectrum, in appeals through religion or black magic or witchcraft for oneness with the universal spirit or god. Others are not so willing participants, as they're dragged kicking and screaming into an alternate consciousness via abduction or getting zapped by beams from above.

In turn, these beings from the superspectrum may need us in some subtle way to exist. They feed on our energy, or recognition or fear, and as a result of this feeding, manifest themselves. Sometimes these beings bring us words of warning, alerting us to heed the need for positive change. It can be a life-enhancing experience, as in a religious conversion. Other beings bring us ill, or induce us to do ill to others, or draw us down a path different from what we have chosen. Their comments are often obscure, or are subtle puns, but if you trace them to their roots, you'll find them potent with meaning. Their methods are inscrutable; their appearances legion.

Cold, Darkly-clothed, Gassy, and Well Heeled

Mothman was not alone. John Keel allowed us, during his unraveling of tales from the Point Pleasant area, to get to know Indrid Cold, too. On Wednesday, November 2, 1966, not far from where the Mothman would begin to haunt the TNT area, sewing-machine salesman Woodrow Derenberger encountered an otherworldly object shaped like "an old-fashioned kerosene lamp chimney, flaring at both ends." Pulling his car to a sudden stop, Derenberger found this strange thing that had plopped itself down in the middle of the Highway 77. Out of the craft and into Derenberger's life stepped this dark-skinned, five-foot-ten-inch-tall man. Smiling, the visitor from elsewhere told Derenberger without moving its lips, that his name was "Indrid Cold." He said he hailed from "a country much less powerful" than the United States.

Soon, the entity got back in the UFO and sped away into the sky. But Cold wasn't through with Derenberger. The salesman was harassed by scary telephone messages, telepathic exchanges, and other staples of what have become known as "Men in Black" encounters. Cold, through thought processes that Derenberger could not explain, told Derenberger that he, Cold, came from the galaxy of Ganymede, specifically the planet Lanulos. Keel chronicled the story and became part of it, experiencing some of the same phone problems and having doppelgangers pose in his place in Point Pleasant. Derenberger would go on to become a famed contactee.

Keel's friend, Point Pleasant newswoman Mary Hyre, also received visits from MIBs of her own. Especially intriguing was her story of the two short men wearing black overcoats who looked almost like twins with dark "Oriental" features. One of them blurted out, "What would you do if someone did order you to stop writing about flying saucers?" Later that same day, another small, Asian-looking man in black visited her office. He had abnormally long fingers and an unfamiliar accent. He introduced himself as "Jack Brown," a UFO researcher, and then stuttered, "What - would - what would you do - if someone ordered - ordered you to stop? To stop printing UFO stories." He denied knowing the other two men but claimed to be a friend of Gray Barker's. A "Jack Brown" also bothered other Point Pleasant witnesses. Gray Barker didn't know a Jack Brown.

Of course, to Keel, Indrid Cold and his MIB clan are nothing more than a human form of the ultraterrestrials he was chasing, or, I should say, who were chasing him. Keel also collected stories of what he called "Grinning Men," big beings that would peer into the windows of the homes of unsuspecting residents. There are other Fortean stories which are variants on the theme. For example, after months of microfilm research, I found all of the original Midwestern articles on the Mad Gasser of Mattoon, Illinois. Then, I tracked down and interviewed eye-witnesses of this cousin of Indrid Cold.

The Mad Gasser terrorized Mattoon during 1944. He or it was described as being tall, dressed in dark clothing, and wearing a tight-fitting cap. The thing would spray a sickeningly sweet gas into the windows of victims homes, causing many to faint. I detailed his reign of mysterious gas attacks in *Mysterious America* (Paraview, 2001). He or it was proceeded by two very similar bedroom invaders in 1934; one was seen in Paris, Missouri, and the other in Botetourt County, Virginia. The Virginian "Gas Thrower," as it was called, had a M.O. which resembled the Mattoon Gasser's, as the marauder would hurl gas into rooms and the local farmers would become violently ill. From December 22, 1933, through January 22, 1934, the attacks were occurring two or three times a week. The "Ghost of Paris" appeared in October, 1934, and was anything but ghostly. He or it was described as tall, thin, and wearing black clothing. It chased children. Here we get a reflective precursor of the May 1981 sightings of the "Phantom Clowns" who attempted to kidnap children throughout the Midwest and the eastern U.S. The traditional black and red clothing of clowns comes out of the portrayal of devils in the Middle Ages. Like Cold, the grinning men, the MIBs, and the Gassers before them, no one ever caught the Phantom Clowns.

The ultimate scary fellow of this kind is Springheel Jack. Again, I've dealt with this entity in *Mysterious America*, but he does deserve to be mentioned with these creepy humanlike "whatevers." Springheel Jack was seen jumping and victimizing women in the dark lanes of Middlesex, England, in November 1837 and February 1838, as well as in 1872 in the Peckham area of southeast London, and April 1877 at Aldershot. He was tall, thin, and had a prominent nose. His bony fingers resembled claws, suggesting immense power. He wore a long, flowing, dark cloak, with a tall, metallic-like helmet on his head. Beneath the cloak were tight-fitting garments of some glittering material like oil-skin or metallic mesh. There appeared from Jack's mouth, according to the 1838 accounts reviewed by Mike Dash in *Fortean Studies* 3, blue flames. Jack's ears were pointed or cropped like the fictional Mr. Spock on "Star Trek." But Springheel Jack was no fiction. He scared and glowed and frightened women, soldiers, and wandering travelers for years. His origins remain a mystery.

Keel believed the MIBs and company were trying to warn us of various things, to predict the assassination of Popes or blackouts or other disasters. Perhaps he was correct and we just haven't been able to read the messages, decode the codes, and demystify the symbols.

For example, one of the more bizarre Men In Black experiences occurred one night in 1976. The details appear below, but curiously at about the same time, around 9:00 PM (Central Time), Mitchell A. Haas, 18, and Joann Sawicki, 18, saw a cigar-shaped object near Racine, Wisconsin. It hovered about 200 yards above the ground, above the Civil Air Patrol building near Highway 20 and West Road, they told sheriff's deputies. The brightly colored object had two pillars extending upward to a platform, on which were three blinking lights. The object came from the southwest, hovered for about three minutes, then left.

Meanwhile, at about the same moment, around 8:00 PM (Eastern Time), an Old Orchard Beach physician named Herbert Hopkins, received a strange phone call from someone who wanted to come over and discuss a UFO incident Hopkins had been investigating. As Hopkins walked to the back door to turn on the porch light, he found the man already coming up the steps. Letting the man in, he noted his strange appearance. He was about five feet, eight inches tall, was bald, and had no eyelashes or eyebrows. He was dressed in a neatly pressed black suit with a black derby hat, black shoes, and a pair of gray gloves. Hopkins noticed that the man was extremely pale, but had ruby red lips, as if he were wearing lipstick.

The man asked Hopkins a number of questions about the Maine

UFO case dealing with an alleged alien abduction case. Hopkins had been performing hypnosis on a young man named David Stephens who claimed to have had numerous encounters with extraterrestrials. The man spoke in a mechanical, monotone voice, without emphasizing any words in his sentences.

Suddenly, the stranger informed Hopkins that there were two coins in Hopkins' pocket and asked him to remove one. Hopkins complied and held the coin, a shiny new penny, in the palm of his hand. The stranger then told Hopkins to watch the coin. Soon, the coin took on a "silvery" appearance and then appeared to be going out of focus, as if it were fading and, eventually, disappeared altogether. The bizarre "ufo investigator" told Hopkins this is what happened to Barney Hill. Barney, of course, is the husband of Betty, and Hopkins knew of the Hill abduction story. The stranger told Hopkins that he was correct that Barney had recently died. "Barney didn't have a heart," said the entity, "just like you no longer have a coin." (Barney Hill died of a cerebral hemorrhage.) The visitor then gently suggested that Hopkins destroy any material he had on the Stephens case. The man stood up, and began talking much slower, and slowly made his way to the door. Seeing a light at the end of his driveway, Hopkins was surprised to see him go in the opposite direction. Hopkins was scared and shaken. That evening Hopkins destroyed his UFO records.

The date in 1976 when a UFO with *two pillars* was sighted in Wisconsin, and a bizarre *stranger visited Maine* before moving on was September 11th.

CHAPTER 8

Flaps: Patterns of Time

John Keel loved to tell the story of a gentle human inhabitant of Earth who was confronted by what he thought was an alien from outer space. The entity kept asking: "What time is it?" I was struck in the wake of the September 11th terror, by a shocking incident involving a Croatian man wrongfully in the U.S. On October 3, 2001, this supposedly deranged illegal alien of a different kind attacked a Greyhound bus driver and caused the vehicle to crash near Hoodoo, Tennessee, killing six people. Yes, Hoodoo, is an early 19th century American term for African-American folk magic, related to voodoo. Before the attack, this man kept asking the passengers of the bus, "What time is it?"

Knowing what time it is seems to be a crude joke. Keel felt it was a clue we could hardly understand. He speculated we were dealing with cosmic jokers. Some of their humor is dark indeed.

My favorite American intellectual of the 1920s once wrote "One measures a circle, beginning anywhere." Charles Fort was correct; everything seems connected.

Twilight Language of the Gods

We ignore, at least psychologically, most of what happens around us. The rationalistic filters allow for only the mundane details of most interactions to awaken any response. In deciphering everything from Mothman sightings to Bigfoot encounters, propelled to our attention via the media or quiet interviews with witnesses, we must look a little deeper.

The missing element in decoding a number of these incidents is an understanding of the story aspect. Nonfiction events in which the outcome may be an encounter are often only viewed in terms of the end result—how many footprints were found, or how bright were the red eyes. The encounters, however, are more than a lone statistic. They are a chain of events, a summary of incidents, which contain the essence of many themes. These motifs are common to influential literature and ancestral traditions, which have imprinted people to such an extent that these stories are passed down from generation to generation.

A story is a message told with words and other symbols, invoking familiar images from the subconscious, which then generate an internal dialogue between our conscious and subconscious. This element must be understood and deciphered if analytic efforts, investigative techniques, and intensive examinations are to be successful. It's useful to read the "twilight language" of these events, before they happen, as well as after the fact.

"Twilight language" concerns, from psychology, the hidden significance of dates and other signs, from religious studies, the hidden symbolism that lies in stories and texts, and from intelligence services work, the profiling insights from specialists that may inform our work. While we do not consciously comprehend the connection, our subconscious may and it is the subconscious that is being addressed, apparently by some of these reports, in a process that CIA behavioral scientist Ewan Cameron terms "psychic driving."

Buddhism's Tantra is thousands of years old, and yet it was never publicly revealed, never written down. Gradually, it became necessary to write the secrets down so they would not be completely lost. But when they were written, they were written in a "twilight language," that is, in allegory, symbolism, code, so they could not be misinterpreted and misused by unworthy seekers. For this reason, if we do not have a proper guide, the ancient texts may be confusing or even misleading to us today.

For all of us who wish to decipher the dates, symbols and twilight language behind the monstrous and mysterious encounters we examine, the "text" may be as difficult to read as that of the ancient Buddhists. Still, we try.

Flaps

Captain Edward Rupert, director of the United States Air Force's Project Blue Book, the government body set aside to study "flying saucers," officially defined the word "flaps." In 1956, Rupert formalized the old military slang for the UFO field when he noted a flap is "a condition or situation, or state of being of a group characterized by an advanced degree of confusion that has not yet reached panic proportions." As Martin Kottmeyer concludes in his article on the subject in *The Anomalist* (Winter 1995–1996)—probably the most intellectual analysis of the subject ever written—flaps are this and more, literally a "crazy time."

Flaps are an attempt to understand a grouping of reports which cluster in time, and for monster accounts, usually in a specific locale. Of particular interest to me are the emotional feelings that "flaps" bring to the Fortean investigations of such reports. Flaps are intense periods of media-driven interest. However, as Kottmeyer points out, the encounters and sightings have to be there for the ridicule curtain, which always exists among the media, to be parted before the reports are published or broadcast. It is not the other way around. The grassroots emotion is there first, then the media follows.

UFO flaps are fairly well-documented, and Jerome Clark has detailed charts of a variety of such occurrences. In general, most UFO authors talk about the major flaps of the late 19th and 20th century as having occurred in 1896, 1897, 1909 (New England), 1912-1913 (UK), 1944-1945, July 1947, July-August 1952, 1954 (France), November 1957, July-August 1965, March-April 1966, November 1966-1967 (West Virginia-Ohio), 1973, 1983 (Hudson Valley, NY), 1987 (Wisconsin), and 1987-1992 (Puerto Rico). Many speculated that there would be many UFOs seen in the skies after the September 11, 2001 terror attacks, when no commercial airlines were flying in the U.S. While an American flap did not materialize, one did take place in Norway.

Flaps are certainly part of the landscape in terms of monster activity as well. Mothman, of course, was one of the more memorable series (November 1966- December 1967) of sightings and related phenomena. The pattern of having a cluster focused in time has been reflected by many cryptid, critter, and creature encounters in North America, some

---

we have investigated and reviewed in this book or others.

In North America, most monster flaps have been concentrated within short periods of times. There have been many. Several examples come to mind:

Nellie the Lion (July 1917) in central Illinois
Mountain Devils (1918, 1924) of Kelso, Washington
Year of the Varmint (1948) in Indiana
The original Bigfoot (October 1958) at Bluff Creek, California
The summer visitors, the Sister Lakes Monster (1964) and
    the Monroe Monster (1965) of Michigan
The Lake Worth Monster (November 1969) of Texas
Momo (July–August 1972), the Missouri Monster
The Farmer City Monster (July 1972) of Illinois
The Big Muddy Monster (June-July 1973) of Murphysboro,
    Illinois
Noxie (September–October 1975) of Oklahoma
Big Birds (March 1976) of the Rio Grande Valley, Texas
Ohio Bigfoot (June–July 1980) of Union and Logan counties
The Scrape Ore Swamp Lizard Man (1988) of South
    Carolina.

During 2000, a major "Bigfoot" flap began at 5:15 AM on March 28, 2000. James Hughes was delivering the little local newspaper, *Black River Shopper*, along County Highway H, near Granton, Wisconsin, when he noticed a figure standing in the ditch and carrying a goat. At first he took it to be a large man, but then he saw it was about eight feet tall and had an ape-like face. The sightings quickly shifted to the Pacific Northwest, and a summer of media attention was devoted to a dozen Sasquatch sightings.

One of the foremost incidents occurred on June 27th, when Gene Sampson found giant footprints behind his home on the Hoh Indian Reservation, near Port Angeles, Washington. Hearing strange "bam, bam" noises, Sampson searched and found two sets of footprints, which he measured at 14 inches and 17½ inches in length, and 7 and 8 inches in width. Cliff Crook, a local Bigfooter, made casts of the prints. While Idaho professor Jeff Meldrum wondered as to the worth of the tracks, Grover Krantz, Bigfoot researcher and retired Washington State University anthropology professor, said he sensed the footprints found on the Hoh reservation indicated one male and one female Sasquatch. But the sightings at the Hoh Reservation were only one of many that had received even-handed publicity out West.

Then on July 1, 2000, the true media storm began when a psychologist reported seeing Bigfoot while hiking, with his family, near the Oregon Caves National Monument, Selma, Oregon. "It was very tall, it was very hairy," Johnson said. "It was nothing else but a Sasquatch. I swear to God. I lived a lot of years in Alaska. I've been chased by a grizzly bear. This was no bear." When Grants Pass psychologist Matthew Johnson says he heard grunts, smelled something musky, and then saw Bigfoot, the press listened, although some Bigfooters were skeptical. The Bigfoot buffs had a difficult time with the media giving so much attention so quickly to someone with a Ph. D., while they had toiled and searched for years and years for evidence without recognition. Johnson's sighting was so fleeting that many wary Bigfooters thought he only had seen a bear.

During September, 2000, Bigfoot researcher Richard Noll and twelve other individuals on an expedition looking for evidence of Bigfoot made a remarkable find, as chance would have it, near Skookum Meadow in the Gifford Pinchot National Forest in southern Washington state. In a mud trap they had created, they obtained a half-body print of a Sasquatch. To attract one of the creatures, the team had set out food, spread pheromones, and played tape recordings thought to be the calls of other Bigfoot. After placing locally grown apples in a muddy spot one evening, the investigators returned the next morning to find an impression which, they concluded, shows the left forearm, hip, thigh and heel of a large primate. They believe the impression was made as the creature sat down and reached over to pick up the bait. The imprint of a hairy buttocks in the mud is the strongest hint yet that Bigfoot is roaming the American Pacific Northwest, according to the Bigfoot Field Researchers Organization, which sponsored the expedition. Anthropologist Jeff Meldrum of Idaho State

University, commented: "All we're trying to say at this stage is that there's evidence that justifies objective consideration." Some critics have commented the imprint is nothing more than an elk body imprint. The study of the cast is ongoing. Thus ended the Summer of the Sasquatch.

Flaps sometimes last a whole year. The year 1973 was called the year of the humanoids among ufologists for the large number of humanlike ufonauts encounters of the third kind, but 1977 was the perhaps most widely explosive year of the past half century in American monsterlore. That one year saw a literal procession of the damned. The Dover Demon visited Dover, Massachusetts. Maned lions attacked dogs in Dover, Arkansas. Black panthers were reported throughout Oklahoma. Mystery cats were sighted in Bay Springs, Mississippi, Edwardsville, Illinois, and California, Kentucky. A black panther killed livestock in Richland Township and Lafayette, Ohio. The "Van Etten Monster" of New York stalked the countryside. Residents of Marlington, West Virginia reported a striped cryptic felid. A twelve-foot hairy apelike creature scared people in Rising Sun, Ohio. Marlon Lowe of Lawndale, Illinois was picked up by a giant thunderbird; the incident set off a flap of big bird sightings. Few years have had such broad-based massive flaps. One wonders if there are cycles underlying any of these flaps.

The late Dr. Frederick Aldrich, a New Brunswick expert on the giant squid, found a thirty-year cycle in giant squid appearances off Newfoundland, with peaks in the 1870s, 1900 to 1910, 1930s, and 1960s. Gary Mangiacopra discovered a similar, if not fainter, cycle for North America sea serpent appearances in the late 1870s, late 1880s, mid-1890s, throughout the period from 1900 to 1910, again starting up in 1929 through the 1930s, and finally with a mini-wave in 1957 to 1964. Is there some relationship between Aldrich's and Mangiacopra's cycles? Perhaps. Aldrich also noted that the giant squids are mostly seen in, and wash ashore during, the autumn. June O'Neill has updated the picture with her book, *The Great New England Sea Serpent*, in which she notes a time gap in sightings for New England. After mentioning the wave of sightings of sea serpents seen off Manchester, Marblehead, and Gloucester, Massachusetts, in 1960, and off Marshfield, Massachusetts, in 1962, O'Neill failed to find any sea serpent activity until the Fortune

Bay, Newfoundland sighting of May 1997. She asks: "Have the creatures returned to the Gulf of Maine after an absence of thirty-five years?" For those tuned into the timing of such things, it was no surprise.

Days, Dates, Months

Do we know what, if any, underlying patterns exist within Mothman, Fortean, and UFO reports? Among creature hunters, there have been attempts to understand their occurrence and timing, usually in terms of hunting down the monsters supposedly responsible. Keel and others have been doing simple analysis since the 1960s, following in the footprints of Charles Fort who loved to look at dates and overlapping phenomena. Creature statistics are often difficult to pin down because the databases are few and far behind.

Looking at well over ten thousand reports of UFOs, John A. Keel came up with some startling findings. In *UFOs: Operation Trojan Horse*, he notes:

> It is obvious that the phenomenon is controlled by hidden laws and cycles. Psychic and occult events seem to follow the same cycles as the UFO phenomenon. The Wednesday-Saturday phenomenon exists in all the frames of reference. For some reason, the twenty-fourth days of April, June, September, November, and December seem to produce exceptional activity year after year....These events are staged year after year, century after century, in the same exact areas and often on the same exact calendar dates. Only the witnesses and the frames of reference used are different.

Commenting on this mysterious timetable, Keel had further comments on the exact periods and places of probable contact:

> So if you are eager to see a genuine example of our phenomenon, pick a good Wednesday or Saturday evening, visit the highest ground in the area closest to you which has a

magnetic fault, and watch the sky around 10:00 PM. The best times are the last two weeks in March and the first two weeks in April, all of July-August, the last two weeks in October, and the first weeks in November and December.

I suspect these guidelines cut across all kinds of phenomena. So you might want to check behind you for a Chupacabras, black dog, or Mothman, if you find yourself on the keel of a hill watching the skies waiting for a UFO.

Others have made similar suggestions. Damon Knight tells of how, while doing research for his book on Charles Fort, he typed twelve hundred file cards containing all the dates and data from Fort's books. What Knight found for the years 1877 to 1892, for example, was that reports of storms, falls, and things seen in space and in the skies all peaked in the same years.

Michael A. Persinger and Gyslaine F. Lafreniere, who developed a theory of geomagnetic interaction and correlationship to Fortean phenomena, fill their book with graphs that have trends similar to those seen by John Green, Gary Mangiacopra, Jerome Clark, Keel, and myself. They show, for instance, that spontaneous human combustions appear to peak in the winter and during April. Forteans have discovered that these time cycles keep showing up across the board.

Monster Months
In June of 1976, John Green, famed Sasquatch chronicler from British Columbia, fed 1,350 Sasquatch/Bigfoot reports into a computer in an attempt to get a portrait of these creatures and their behaviors. He was able to discover some composites, but, in general, he was frustrated by the effort. After discussing this attempt in his book, *Sasquatch: The Apes Among Us,* he writes:

> Anyone trying seriously to make some sense out of this is probably fuming by now; because you obviously don't learn much unless you can relate things like time of day, time of year, type of location, geographic location, activity of the

witness, etc., and find consistent patterns. If the weather, the altitude, and the phase of the moon would fit in too, that would be even better. That is the sort of thing we tried to do with the computer, and I have spent many a day at it with pencil and paper. I have made charts that will tell what the witness was doing, the type of locale, the season, the time of day, whether it was forested or open, what decade it was, approximately how high, in what state, whether there was snow on the ground, and whether there were tracks found, all from a single entry. I also have maps marked to show what was seen, what time of day, what time of year, by whom, how long ago, how high, and whether there was snow on the ground. They don't show any useful pattern at all. What they do show is that the patterns some people claim to have found—migration routes for instance—just aren't there.

Nonetheless Green was able to come up with some amazing general remarks about patterns. "The most common type of report in British Columbia is a Sasquatch seen on the beach from a boat in the daytime," Green observed. Looking at seasons, he found "the most common form of sighting is by someone driving on a side road, in the fall, in California or Washington." That information came from computer sorting of the data, but I think that this man's sense of the phenomena is just as impor- tant. He writes: "Actually the people with the best mathematical chance to see a Sasquatch are almost certainly those who sit up nights where skunk apes have been reported garbage hunting in western Florida, and after that would come anyone who regularly drives the road to Easterville in northern Manitoba—but I didn't learn those things from statistics."

Other Bigfoot researchers have had feelings about the patterns of the sightings, and sometimes they involved the phases of the moon. Shortly before he died, George Haas, founder of the *Bigfoot Bibliography* told me that he had strong evidence that most of the north- ern California encounters occurred during the new moon. Some Bigfooters have related this to the "dark of the moon" hunting behavior of some larger animals; others don't know what it means. Green found that the pre-1970 reports were mainly daytime sightings, but he had seen a dramatic shift in the timing of reports occurring in southern California and the eastern United States by the mid-1970s. "The vast majority are at night," wrote Green.

The Extremes of April and May

One anomaly John Green seems especially troubled by is the very low number of sightings during one particular month. "The puzzling thing," he wrote, "…is the low total for May, which is quite consistent geographically…If there is a month when Sasquatch head for the high country or the deep bush, May is apparently it. Perhaps they are shy creatures and May is the mating season. I don't know anything on the human side of the situation to explain it. Possibly it is just accidental and will disappear when more reports are in, but it doesn't seem likely."

Interestingly, Green's May anomaly agrees with the evidence coming out of other monster cycles. Analyzing all the phantom panther reports I've gathered from the east for the years 1900 to 1970, I was struck by how they seemed to clump in the winter months of November, December, and January; and in the summer and fall months of June, July, August, and September. August had the most number of sightings; May the least. Graphically speaking, May appeared to be in a valley between some very high frequencies for April and the beginning of the summer curve in June.

Gary Mangiacopra's results for the Northeast's sea serpent sightings tend to agree with what Green and I have found. Systematically searching through six daily newspapers for the years 1869 to 1976, Mangiacopra surveyed just over 640 years of news, page by page—a truly monumental effort. "Roughly three-fourths of all sightings were occurring during the summer months," Mangiacopra noted. "The remaining one-fourth was occurring during the fall and winter months, during the time of which one would generally assume sightings would not be reported."

So what happened to the spring sightings? Before the turn of the century, Mangiacopra could not find one sea serpent report for March, April, or May. During the entire period of his search, he discovered July, followed by August, were the high reporting months. Why are monsters seen less often in the late spring in North America, when, with more people coming outside to enjoy the warmer weather, you would expect more sightings?

Even the thunderbirds, as I noted earlier in this book, tend to be seen on either side of May, with highs mainly for April and in the summer. Out-of-place alligators, discussed in *Mysterious America* (2001), also show this dislike for May. Michael A. Persinger and Gyslaine F. Lafreniere also comment on this timing issue in their massive work on Fortean patterns, *Space-Time Transient and Unusual Events.* "Conspicuously," they noted, "the unknown flying creature subcategory peaks in April for the years analyzed."

More April Reappearances

A phenomenon similar to spook lights—those globes of ghostly illumination that are seen over and over in one location, according to local traditions—is the phantom train phenomenon, which appear to witnesses at recurring intervals and seems to repeat the April pattern we find elsewhere. Some of these reappearances are quite elaborate. Take, for example, the frequent sightings of Lincoln's funeral train. According to an article from the 1920s, in the Albany, New York, *Evening Times:*

> Regularly in the month of April, about midnight the air on the tracks becomes very keen and cutting. On either side of the tracks it is warm and still. Every watchman, when he feels the air, slips off the track and sits down to watch. Soon the pilot engine of the Lincoln's funeral train passes with long, black streamers and with a band of black instruments playing dirges, grinning skeletons sitting all about.
>
> It passes noiselessly. If it is moonlight, clouds come over the moon as the phantom train goes by. After the pilot engine passes, the funeral train itself with flags and streamers rushes past. The track seems covered with black carpet, and the coffin is seen in the center of the car, while all about it in the air and on the train behind are vast numbers of blue-coated men, some with coffins on their backs, others leaning upon

them.

If a real train were passing its noise would be hushed as if the phantom train rode over it. Clocks and watches always stop as the phantom train goes by and when looked at are five to eight minutes behind. Everywhere on the road about April 27 watches and clocks are suddenly found to be behind.

The ghost of Lincoln's funeral train illustrates the revisitations of such phenomena. A common factor of the reappearing phantom trains is their tragic tone. Trains and stretches of track involved in deaths, accidents, and wrecks are the ones that foster the periodically repeating ghosts. And the phantom trains may have a corner on the twenty-sevenths of April as well. I note the Ghost of the Statesville, North Carolina wreck reappears on April 27th, too.

A Special Day

While April is "hot," filled with everything from last century's reports of airships and phantom trains to the recent accounts of flying men and giant birds, in terms of intrigue, one of the most long-lasting timing issues is associated with a specific date—June 24th.

June 24th is St. John's Day. The feast of St. John the Baptist is one of the oldest, if not *the* oldest, to be introduced into the liturgies of the Greek and Latin churches in a saint's honor. But instead of celebrating the saint's day on the day of his death, as is customary, this day is remembered for St. John's birth. St. John is invoked against hail (please note, falling ice), epilepsy, convulsion, and spasms. (The man himself, John the Baptist, is seen as the forerunner, cousin, and baptizer of Jesus. Living in the wilderness, he is portrayed as a mystic who lived on a diet of locusts and wild honey [see Matthew 3]. His beheading is frequently depicted in Christian art.)

St. John's Day was long associated in Europe with the midsummer festivities. On St. John's Eve fires were built on every hill, following the old custom of lighting Beltane fires dedicated to the god Bel or Baal. (Although "Beltane," per se, is May 1st, the fires lit at all lunar and solar festivals are often referred to as "Beltane fires.")

The Irish and English once believed that on St. John's Eve the soul of every person left their body, found the place where they would die, and then returned to the body. A person sitting on a church porch all night fasting would see passing before him all the local people who would die during the coming year. In many ways, these traditions are akin to those of Halloween in which the souls of the dead circulate in graveyards.

As Janet and Colin Bords note in their excellent book, *Earth Rites*, St. John's Day/Midsummer Day is associated with dancing around a birch tree in a fashion not unlike the fertility rites of dancing about the maypole on May Day. They observe that the tree can be regarded as the earth phallus, "the male principle jutting out of the earth," while the other is like a "fruit-bearing tree of life," which is female.

Fairies, the Occult, and June 24th

The pagan custom of bathing and round dances on St. John's Eve was forbidden by the church in an effort to stamp out the fertility rites of the past. Likewise the collecting of the glowworms and the luminous St. John's wort (which has seen a reemergence in alternative medical treatments in the 21st century) occurred through the night beginning on St. John's Eve. The wort was seen as equal protection against the devil and from abduction by fairies. ("Pagan" is a word with origins in the movement to dismiss earth rites' impact and import in everyday living. Pagan merely means rural.)

Obviously, the rural festivals marking the summer solstice and midsummer's day had to be dealt with by the church, and St. John's Day was created. However, the wonder of this special time, acknowledged by these past peoples so deeply in tune with Gaia, has not been so easily diminished.

Elizabethan England felt the date was important when fairies and the little people were said to be around and about. Shakespeare's *A Midsummer Night's Dream*, with its rich lore of the fairy, Puck, or Robin Goodfellow is familiar to many, but few nowadays recall its relationship to June 24th.

Adepts in the occult have long been aware of the significance of the day, and have used the "power" of the date to conjure new ventures. King Edward Ill of England, a great follower of the legendary King Arthur and the Round Table, founded The Order of the Garter on June 24, 1348. In 1633 on June 24th the Inquisition released Galileo. In 1717, the Grand Lodge of Freemasons was inaugurated in London. By tradition this is the date in the thirteenth century when the Pied Piper of Hamelin returned, piping his haunting tune, which convinced 130 children into following him from town to a mountain, never to be seen again. This was, literally, an enchanted kidnapping on a grand scale.

An early American utopian community known as the "Woman of the Wilderness" was entwined with St. John's Day. Sailing from Germany on February 13, 1694, they arrived at their destination, Germantown, Pennsylvania on June 24th of the same year, and immediately burned St. John's bonfires, made ritual incantations, and called on heavenly powers to sanctify their new home. The group was an interesting mixture of believers in Primitive Christianity, Theosophy, Rosicrucianism, and paganism; they were energetic musicians and active educators, and were responsible for the first volume of music published in America.

During the seventh anniversary of the Woman of the Wilderness' arrival, a curious incident occurred. According to Mark Holloway's *Heavens on Earth*, just as members of the community were about to light their bonfire, "a white, obscure, moving body in the air attracted their attention, which, as it approached, assumed the form and mien of an angel. It receded into the shadows of the forest and appeared again immediately before them as the fairest of the lovely." Holloway notes they fell to their knees and prayed but "their angel vanished, without so much as a word of good cheer." This encounter overlaps with many accounts we have studied of UFOs, religious visions, and angelic ufonauts (see my first book, *The Unidentified*) and significantly took place on June 24, 1701.

More recently, investigators of the unexplained have sensed something was different about this date. Charles Fort wrote of a mysterious jellylike mass that was found covering the ground at Eton, Bucks, England in 1911 on June 24h. And in true Fortean fashion there are a couple of falls for 1877: a red rain fell on parts of Italy on St. John's Eve, and huge pieces of ice dropped from the sky at Fort Lyon, Colorado on June 24th.

Even bizarre disappearances focus on this date. According to the Soviet newspaper *Pravda*, a freight train, with twenty-eight cars carrying crushed rocks, left the factory in Tomashgrodsky, U.S.S.R. on June 24, 1983, never to be seen again. "It left, but it never arrived," the Russian press commented.

The Significance of June 24, 1947

For ufologists this date is of critical importance. On June 24, 1947 the modern era of UFOs began with Kenneth Arnold's dramatic sighting of "saucers" flying between Mount Rainier and Mount Adams in Washington. Because of the primary significance of this particular date, however, searching more broadly into other events occurring on that day appears to reveal some hidden connections to St. John's Day.

The headline news event for June 24, 1947 (obviously published in the next day's papers) was the beginning of a massive coal miner's strike in the U.S. (Coal men, of course, have always been associated, traditionally, with the burning of the Beltane and beacon fires of old, along ley lines. UFOs, literally "fires in the skies," some writers believe, "travel" the ley lines.) We find the news of June 24, 1947 filled with reports of fires. A large fire in Brussels killed seventeen when a stock of film mysteriously and spontaneously exploded and trapped five hundred people, for a time, in a building. A huge fire in Perth Amboy, New Jersey destroyed a department store and caused the evacuation of two adjoining movie theaters. A big fire was reported in London. A United Air Lines plane traveling from Chicago to Cleveland was struck and burned by a bolt of lightning. Fire equipment waited on the ground, but the plane landed safely.

With St. John's Day named after a man who ate locusts and wild honey, we note, in a bizarre twist of fate, that on June 24, 1947 the nations of Guatemala and El Salvador were said to be using fire in the form of flame-throwers to destroy hordes of grasshoppers invading their countries. Meanwhile, back in Washington, where Kenneth Arnold was experiencing and telling about a UFO sighting that would greatly impact the future, a

Katherine Moseley of Seattle was being stung to death by wasps or bees. (Perhaps the name game is at play here too, as the years since 1947 have seen a James Moseley become one of the foremost figures in ufology. Moseley's personal and folksy style has made his name a buzzword in the field. He is a popular figure among hundreds of flying saucer buffs.)

UFO Deaths and Connections to St. John's Day

UFO writers John Keel and the late Otto Binder (1911-1975, and most famous for *UFOs Are Watching Us*) noticed a number of "seemingly coincidental deaths in the UFO field on 24 June." These included in 1964 Frank Scully, author of one of the first crashed-saucer books; British contactees Arthur Bryant and Richard Church in 1967; and Willy Ley in 1969. Frank Edwards, popular UFO author and radio personality in the 1950s, died a few hours before Bryant. News of the sudden death of Frank Edwards stunned delegates assembled for the 1967 Congress of Scientific Ufologists in New York City's Hotel Commodore on June 24th.

June twenty-fourths have had their share of weird UFO accounts since 1947, as well. For example, in 1953 a gigantic UFO with a series of red lights and portholes was seen over Hampton Bay, Long Island. While it flew backwards over water, it made "the same noise as a swarm of bees!" Two days later a "yellowish moss" was found at the site. The connections between the elements of this report and the bees/honey of St. John seem quite obvious. As Jerry Clark and I stated in our 1975 book, *The Unidentified*, many fairy witnesses hear the sound of buzzing flies or bees. Speaking of UFOs, we wrote: "Contactees occasionally remark on the 'bee-buzzing' sound at the beginning and/or conclusion of their encounters." In Orphic tradition, the bee had a deep, spiritual importance. Human souls were said to travel in swarms, like swarms of bees. The grasshopper or locust, likewise, travels in swarms and held symbolic significance in ancient times; for example, the golden locust is the emblem of the sun god Apollo.

Furthermore, ambrosia, the thick, syrupy, honey-like food of the gods, fairies, and little people, often given to mortal men, shares traits with these stories. Ambrosia, in more modern times, appears to have turned up as the Long Island yellowish moss of June 24, 1953, the jelly masses found at Eton on June 24, 1911, and the traditional June 24 yellow St. John's wort so often associated with protection from the fairies.

UFOs and this day have a long-shared history that continues to the present. On June 24, 1954, R. B. Tomer, director of engineering for CBS-Hytron, saw a white, elliptical UFO above Danvers, Massachusetts. On June 24, 1985, over northern and central Florida, a string of bright lights swept across the sky prompting thousands of phone calls from people alarmed about UFOs. As recently as June 24, 2000, in Wintersville, Ohio, witnesses saw a large cylinder shaped object with what appeared to be a wing in the middle. The object had pale orange spots and made no sound. It cast a feathery blur as it angled off to the north. On June 24, 2001, southern Russian officials reported that puzzled farmers from the village of Yuzhnove, near Stavropol, saw a UFO land in a barley field.

And Monsters Too

Strange monster accounts have turned up on St. John's Day, as well. A few examples demonstrate the bizarre nature of the cases. In the midst of a series of winged vampire cat incidents in Ontario, on June 24, 1966, one of these critters was apparently pumped full of bullets in the village of Alfred. A flap of Bigfoot-like creature sightings in Logan and Union Counties, Ohio took place in 1980, the strangest of which was the encounter reported by Union County legal secretary Mrs. Donna Riegler. The Bords note:

> She was driving home from work on 24 June: It was a stormy evening after a hot, muggy day. Lightning flickered, the sky darkened, and large drops of rain began to fall, but Mrs. Riegler had no inkling of what was about to happen. She told a reporter: "I was in a good mood. I just wanted to get home. I went over the railroad tracks slow. I always do because I don't want to knock my wheels out of line. Then I saw this thing laying on the road, hunched over. I thought it was a dog at first. Then it stood up, and I thought it was a

man. I thought he was crazy, laying on the road. I couldn't figure why he was out there. He had no golf clubs. No luggage; Then he turned around and looked at me." When asked for more details of the creature's appearance, she demonstrated its posture: upright, with knees bent, and hands held out, palms up. She could not see any facial features. Mrs. Riegler escaped as fast as she could, stopping at a stranger's house where, unnerved by her experience, she broke down and sobbed.

And during the flap of 2000, Sasquatch footprints were found at Olympic National Park, in Washington state, along the Sol Duc River— on June 24th.

Predictions

We care about patterns because people are interested in predicting the behavior of the phenomena. Predictions are a dangerous thing. Sometimes they come true. Sometimes they don't.

In 1998, the web edition of *The Anomalist* (www.anomalist.com) published a feature article entitled "Still Waiting: A List of Predictions from the 'UFO Culture'" by Martin S. Kottmeyer. In it, the author looks at what he calls "Fetridge's Law," which is named after an unfortunate media personality named Fetridge who ambitiously decided to do a live broadcast of the return of the swallows to Capastrano. Of course, that year the swallows decided to come late. "Fetridge's Law" thus states: "Important things that are supposed to happen do not happen, especially when people are watching you."

Kottmeyer then penned a long essay on predictions, gleamed from the UFO literature. Most of which failed. Kottmeyer's superb analysis of Keel's predictions from the time of the Mothman visitations, 1966-1967, is an excellent summary of Keel's deciphering of "twilight language":

John Keel's extraordinary odyssey through the UFO phenomenon climaxes in a series of prophecies related by contactees and purportedly originating from an entity named Apol. The style and atmosphere of Keel's books cannot be captured by mere iteration of the events reported by him. One feels like a vandal trying to offer a summary like the following chronology, but it would be a greater crime not to include some sort of account of so important an example of this phenomenon.

May 1967: Silent contactees predict giant power failure.

June 5, 1967: A massive power failure occurs in the Northeast USA. Its scope is less than the 1965 Blackout.

June 19: Apol predicts things will get more serious in the Middle East. The Pope will go there on a peace mission and be knifed to death. Then, the Anti-Christ will rise up out Israel. Apol adds the Vatican would send food and aid to refugees.

June 21: Keel hears by way of another ufologist that a famous newsman in the Midwest would soon die.

June 23: Frank Edwards, a newscaster and author of two flying saucer books, dies of heart failure in Indiana.

June 28: The Vatican announces they are sending assistance to war victims. Apol and others step up their warnings about the Pope. They add a man in a black suit with a black knife would attack him in an airport. More predictions warn of impending plane crashes and Robert Kennedy being in grave danger.

Also in June: In the wake of '67 Blackout, there is a warning a yet bigger power failure would happen. This would be followed by natural catastrophes. New York City would slide into the Ocean on July 2. Rumors spread and hardware stores sell out of candles and flashlights. Keel, himself, stocks up on water.

July 2: Nothing.

.

July 20: The Vatican announces the Pope will visit Turkey. Contactees date his assassination for the 26th. They add it would be preceded by an earthquake and followed by three days of darkness.

July 22: A deadly earthquake hits Turkey.

July 25: The Pope lands in Istanbul.

July 26: The Pope leaves Istanbul. The visit is without incident. Keel however does see UFOs on this date. Ha-ha-ha. Undaunted, Apol and company predicts a new big event for December 15. They also predict the dollar would be devalued (No), Red China would join the U.N. (Yes), and Keel would move to a New York apartment on the ground floor. They also foretell a terrible disaster on the Ohio River - people will die. They imply a plant will blow up. With time, details of the December 15 event fill in. Space people would time a countrywide blackout to happen the moment Lyndon Johnson lit the White House Xmas tree. Considering this the sort of thing those perverse aliens would do for yuks, Keel buys into this prediction, albeit warily, and prepares for a blackout.

October: "Hopi and Navaho Indians will make headlines shortly before Xmas."

December 16–26: There is a rescue effort to help Southwest Indian reservations hit by a snowstorm. Among them are Navaho and Hopi.

December 15: LBJ throws the switch. Immediately comes news that a bridge along the Ohio River has collapsed during rush hour. Keel had crossed that bridge many times in the past. People died.

December 17: The Prime Minister of Australia goes for a swim in rough surf and his body vanishes. This was predicted, says Keel.

December 18: An Air Force jet plows into a Tucson shopping center. Keel indicates this was predicted the day before. (This is incorrectly dated in his account as December 11.)

Undated: An unprecedented event is scheduled for

December 24. A great light will appear in the sky and then....

December 24, 1967: Nothing

June 6, 1968: Robert Kennedy assassinated.

November 27, 1970: A man dressed in black and wielding a kris, a black knife, attacks the Pope in an airport. Not Istanbul: Manila International Airport. Benjamin Mendoza AMR Flores, a surrealist painter, was outfitted in a priest's cassock to do the deed. An art critic commented that Flore's art was contrived, but betrayed no madness. Those familiar with Keel's concept of reprogrammed humans doing things in the name of the phenomenon may be puzzled to find Flores had no voices in his head egging him on. His act was in opposition to hypocrisy and superstition - an act of ideology. On September 2 of that same year an individual who had been hearing voices in his head did attack the Pope, but with stones.

Keel interprets all this as some sort of perverse game to lure people in and then make them appear foolish when they have people's attention. Acceptable, but one could alternatively interpret this pattern as a working out of Fetridge's Law. It is always the most important events that fail to live up to expectations.

September 11th, 2001, will be forever linked to tragic anniversary memories for generations to come. After the terror happened, I received various emails from Forteans mentioning that there appeared to be an upsurge in strange animal reports *after* the 9/11 events. I had to point out, however, that each and every one of the curious encounters people were discussing had actually happened right *before* the horrific events of September 11th. The stories included reports of an eight-foot tall "monkey" being seen in New Hampshire early on the 11th, and a black panther stalking rural Elkhart County, Indiana on the 9th and 10th of September, 2001.

Banshees apparently still exist.

CHAPTER 9

Windows: Patterns of Place and Name

Certain areas appear to be routinely visited by Fortean events. Depending upon your interests, these locales may be called "haunted places," "monster countries," "spook light sites," "triangles," or "windows." John Keel created the concept and indeed coined the word, as well as certainly popularizing the notion of "windows" when he first talked about them menacingly and humorously in his articles and books of the 1970s. Although he introduced the idea in *UFOs: Operation Trojan Horse* in 1970, most people relate the term "window" to the area around Point Pleasant, West Virginia, and Keel's book about it, *The Mothman Prophecies* (1975).

"The phenomena he records," wrote Jerome Clark in *High Strangeness* (1996), "exemplify the window at its bizarre best: Over a period of many months UFO activity is frequent, sometimes so frequent that people go UFO-hunting on a nightly basis with reasonable expectations of sighting something. The sightings include events ranging from distant observations to close encounters. Paranormal activity of other sorts often amplifies as well; the Point Pleasant area was also a hotbed for encounters with men in black and a monstrous creature known as Mothman. This full panoply of phenomena accompanies some long-term, narrow-distribution waves; in others the window opens wide enough to admit only UFOs."

Not everyone has been happy with Keel's notion of windows. As Hilary Evans pointed out in *Fortean Times:* "Insofar as Keel has encouraged serious and thoughtful researchers to extend their notions of the possible, he can have done nothing but good. Insofar as has encouraged flightier minds to espouse dubious notions for which the evidence is less than adequate, he may have done more harm than good."

Therefore, as we venture forth, searching for monsters and in mini-malls for crypto cultural artifacts (i.e. tourist trinkets reflecting the local natives capturing of a permanent or transitory phenomenal visitation or event), let us do it with caution. Some window areas like Gulf Breeze, Florida, may have more to do with the publicity machine of a local advocate of dubious UFO activity than the actual worthiness of the site. Sedona, Arizona, is another "new age" vortex that may have more to do with marketing than Forteana. Some supposed spooky sites that I will give no time to at all here are "mystery spots" and "magnetic hills" which are straightforward optical illusions. Others such as Bluff Creek, California, fifty miles deep into the wilderness, are not for the faint of heart and certainly are not a tourist trap.

As you examine "window" areas, you will soon discover that within North America, all states and provinces can boast from two to twelve such locales, where phenomena will repeatedly appear and reappear.

Window areas exist elsewhere around the world, of course. Certain authors, following in the Keelian tradition, have done their homework and fieldwork in chronicling these windows. For instance, Jon Downes in his books (*The Owlman and Others*, 1998; *Only Fools and Goatsuckers*, 1999; *The Rising of the Moon*, 1999) detailed a wide variety of winged weirdies, sky objects, monsters, phantom cats, black dogs, and other of what he calls "zooform" phenomena, from Puerto Rico to the United Kingdom to Hong Kong. Downes has noted, in particular, the 1976 flap which centered on Cornwall in the United Kingdom, and specifically pinpointing the Mothman-like episodes of the Owlman as being tied to the Mawnam Old Church. Downes and Scott Corrales (*Chupacabras and Other Mysteries*, 1997) have both linked the red-eyed, winged, and spiky wonders to certain special places in Puerto Rico and Mexico.

Haunted Attachments

Windows areas have many ways of presenting themselves and even more names for people to place upon them. Sometimes the window appears to be "open" all the time. Spook light and ghost light sites demonstrate a fixed location with a long history of activity. Spook lights are formally defined as mysterious, usually mobile globes of illumination seemingly attached to, and appearing periodically at specific locations.

A sample of the more famous spook lights, which often have monikers reflecting their locations, include the Brown Mountain Lights (North Carolina), Joplin Spooklight (Missouri-Kansas-Oklahoma line), Big Thicket Ghost Light (Texas), and the Hebron Light (Maryland).

At various times railroad lights, a special form of spook lights, indicate a haunted attachment in another way. In terms of spookiness, perhaps nothing can challenge the lone wailing of a distant train in the empty air of a quiet rural setting. As the listener strains to hear the next banshee-like screech of the iron monster, the eyes try to pick out the faraway beam of light from the headlamp of the expected train. But people have waited for just such a slowly approaching train, only to then hear a ghost engine crash or see passing in front of them a haunting shell of unreal railroad coaches and their skeletal passengers. Observers who search for a trace of the wreckage, never find it. The witnesses are especially baffled.

Phantom trains are heard and seen from one end of the globe to the other, but no one can easily explain the source of the phenomenon. From Burma, reports of a phantom train heard blowing its whistle, steaming along, and then crashing from the fallen River Kwai Bridge circulated in 1958. Prisoners of war who worked on the railway said they had heard the ghost train since shortly after the British bombed the bridge, knocking a Japanese train into a ravine below. Often the permanent phenomena is tied to an old story of a wreck or tragic end.

Humans are rational beings needing explanations for why they see strange things, and oftentimes, the answers come through a cultural context. The ghosts of wrecked trains are one fashionable way to deal with spook lights seen near railroad tracks. Sometimes locals remain attached to this "explanation" even after the tracks have been removed.

Exactly such a circumstance was revealed in March 1951 at Suffolk in Nansemond County, Virginia. After several people saw what was labeled "The Light," investigating Deputy Sheriff Hurley Jones saw it, too. He described The Light as resembling a single automobile head-lamp seen head-on. Jeston Reid, 62, who lives on Jackson Road, informed investigators at the time that his father told him he saw the spook light in the late 1870s. Raleigh Outland stated he had seen it all his life. He noted that sometimes it stays "right in the middle of the road, about five feet off the ground," and at other times veers off to the side of Jackson Road. The head of the state troopers locally, Sergeant W.S. Dameron, said: "It's a bright light that looks exactly like a train coming down a track."

Over three hundred cars showed up in March of 1951, truly a flap situation, looking for an answer to the mystery of The Light. Serious investigations into the matter brought forth the discovery that the old Jackson and Whaleyville Railroad ran down the strip that has since been renamed the Jackson Road. Deputy Sheriff Beale, 75, recalled that a railroad flagman was killed on the line, in about 1912, and many folks believed it was the flagman with his lantern that was haunting the old railroad bed. But general agreement in Suffolk County is that the light had been seen long before that occurrence.

We find phantom train reports especially interesting in a Keelian way, for one major reason. They stay put and appear to be grounded at a window site. The phantom trains tend to be analogous to spook lights found in rural areas, to UFOs that frequently visit UFO windows, or even to the ghosts that haunt certain houses, because of their seeming loyalty to one particular spot. The phantom trains are likewise mysteri-ous mobile lights attached to a specific location, but they also seem to manifest other characteristics, such as making noises.

Theories of about spook lights and location-specific ghost train lights often center on magnetic anomalies that abound around such sites. Keel and others have found merit in such speculation. But paranormal or psychic theories have also been considered over the years. So very many spook lights have occurred along or near railroad tracks that the com-mon folkloric explanation is that the light is the swinging lantern of a dead trainman. This is the explanation given for the origin of the New Jersey mystery light, although C. Louis Weidemann of the Vestiga group, firmly accepts an electromagnetic origin to such things.

In touring the country, I too have heard the ghostly explanation first and foremost from railroad spook light sites in the East to ghostly haunted railroad trestles in the West. Rural and urban folklore, of course, tend to drift in this direction. Psychic investigators tend to explain spook lights in terms of deceased spirits; apparently phantom trains could also be viewed as ghost objects of the past.

Mounds and Fort

Areas associated with Indians and their stories also tend to be window areas. Gregory Little in *People of the Web* links mounds and phenomena because "there are certain areas spread over the earth that were recognized as 'different' by the ancients because strange things happened there." Nothing could be more permanent that the mounds and stoned forts found around the world which evidence some window activity; Moundsville, West Virginia's 1890s involvement in mysterious airship activity was followed by a century of strange events.

I have journeyed far since 1960, to find these weird places, but sometimes they have been in my back yard. I fell in love with southern Illinois when I first traveled there, in particular its smoothly rolling hills and calm vistas. The first time I went looking for the stone forts of the area, I remember vividly topping the crest of a small upheaval in the land and being greeted with a burst of yellow from a vast field of daffodils. The beauty of this land, which has more in common with areas south of the Mason-Dixon line than its Yankee history might indicate, would be enough to fill anyone with wonder. But the mysteries of the region make it a doubly enchanting place to explore. And many before me had viewed this anomaly, that is, the stone forts.

Since the late eighteenth century, the stone forts of southern Illinois have been a mystery to the immigrant Europeans and Africans. Colonel Leonard White noted the walls when he toured the region shortly after the Revolutionary War. Down through the years, discussions of the forts have continued in obscure historical society journals, and spoken of in the 1930s when the Shawnee National Forest was developed and people were able to explore the ancient hollows and rock shelters. This section of Illinois has the unique feature of being called "Egypt" or "Little Egypt," adding another level of intrigue to the story–a Masonic one, as it turns out—which would be interwoven into the mystery of the "ancient ones." Over and over again the wondrous nature of the structures was discussed because, simply, no one knew what to make of them.

During the 1930s, at least ten pre-Columbian stone forts were found to exist in the hills of southern Illinois. But by 1996, the situation had changed dramatically. Mark Wagner, director of the Center for Archaeological Investigations at Southern Illinois University, would write on the center's website: "For years, there was only 17 known sites in southern Illinois, yet across the river in Missouri, they had several hundred sites. Within the last few years, we've probably added 20 additional sites."

There may be other forts in southern Illinois, the walls of which have been razed down to ground level; one of the more recent finds was made when the foundation courses were accidentally observed. These chance finds have many people wondering if the known walls are just the tip of the iceberg. The researchers from Southern Illinois University think there is a strong probability that several smaller walls may exist in the remote backwash of the Shawnee National Forest, an area of concentrated weirdness ranging from sightings of Bigfoot-type creatures and phantom panthers to the usual run of UFO stories. Of the ten original mystery walls located in the 1930s, most of them are to be found near the Devil's Kitchen area.

Devil's Names

I've been writing about the "name game" since my first article in 1972, on devil's names and Fortean places for *Fortean Times*. I explored the concept again in *Mysterious America*, reinforcing the notion that early settlers found certain locations "strange" and called them "devil" places to acknowledge those feelings.

During the 1980s, having collected 125 places with "devil names" in the United States, I noticed that some regions had more than others. New England is a hot area, because of its colonial history. The home state of the Salem witch trials, Massachusetts, for example, had an early tradition of naming many spots after the evil one. Some of these include:

Devil's Pulpit on Monument Mountain
Devil's Den, Newbury
Devil's Den, a cave in northern Hampshire County
Devils Football, on Mt. Holyoke
Devil's Mouth Cave, near Westwood
Devil's Cartway and Devil's Oven, near Sherborn
Devil's Den, in Needham, near Dover
Devil's Footprint, in Norton
Devil's Den, in Williamsburg
Devil's Den Cave
Salem Witch's Caves, at Ashland

Henry Franzoni, a Sasquatch researcher living in the Pacific Northwest with a remarkable names database, told me that as of 1998, he had found 2,635 places named (or which were named) Devil, Diablo, or Diabla in the United States.

Other subtler examples still come to my attention. The areas named Hockomock—a peninsula and bay in Maine, a swamp and cemetery in Massachusetts, and other sites throughout New England—all have been associated with UFOs, strange lights, bizarre creatures, ghosts, disappearances, and the like. Hockomock, as well as its related forms, is an Algonquian word for "evil spirit" or "devil." One of these, the Hockomock Swamp, which comprises the largest vegetated freshwater wetland system in Massachusetts, is called the Bridgewater Triangle by modern locals (see *Mysterious America*). It is a place where people vanish and creatures like giant snakes, Bigfoot, Thunderbirds, and phantom panthers are seen. I first talked to Hockomock-area residents and Native Americans about the meaning of the name "Hockomock" to discover its link to the word "Devil," and another variant, "Hoccomocco," which means or "evil spirit." George R. Stewart's *American Place Names* (NY: Oxford University Press, 1970) relates the words "Hobomak, Hobbomoc, Hobbomocka [as] Algonquian, with reference to an evil spirit or the idea of a place being haunted; by the colonists taken to be 'the Indian devil,' [the name is found in connection to] several features in New England." (p. 207)

Skeptics of my arguments regarding devil-named places point to

Anglo-Americans' expectations of something bizarre happening at a "Devil's Den," or "Devil's Kitchen." But what are we to make of the phenomenon that most local Hockomock residents, who do not understand the name has evil connotations, continue to experience concentrated waves of weird events in these places?

Other similar Native American words, like Manitou, have been used to label the "bedeviled places" and hint at a long-term knowledge of what I've called "Keel's Children" that haunt these spots.

And then there's Skookum. Remember the flap called the "Summer of the Sasquatch" in 2000? At it's end (no pun intended), Richard Noll found the so-called butt print of a Sasquatch. Jeff Meldrum of Idaho State University, in a story published in *New Scientist* (December 23, 2000) noted that the imprint seems to have been made by a large, hair-covered hominid more than seven and a half feet tall. Meldrum found markings that look like human dermal patterns (such as those found on human feet) on the heel print. They found it near Skookum Meadow in the Gifford Pinchot National Forest in southern Washington State.

Intriguingly, Henry Franzoni's interest in the name game goes back to his first experience with the unknown in 1993. At a place called Skookum Lake, Oregon, Franzoni and his companion encountered what he would later call the "Bigfoot phenomenon." Franzoni began collecting Native tales, and started noticing the links between the "name game" of the locations' names and the sightings of the creatures. Not coincidentally, Franzoni discovered that "Skookum" was another name for Sasquatch or Bigfoot. He has identified 214 "Skookum" place names in Oregon, Washington State, British Columbia, Idaho, and Alaska.

Franzoni wrote me about "Skookum" in 1999:

> The modern Chinook jargon meaning is "big, strong, and swift" whilst the original Chinook village meaning is "Evil God of the Woods." Places have to be examined as to when they were named, and often a correlating old story has to be located to really suggest that a particular Skookum place is worthy of our Bigfoot interest. A number of Skookum places fit the bill just fine after being investigated

though. Places like Mt. Duckabush in the Olympic Range was once named "Mt. Arleta" by Lt. Patrick O'Neill, who led the second group ever across the Olympic Mountains in 1890. O'Neill mentioned in his diary that the native guides he had with him called it "Skookum" and believed their gods lived on it. His native guides abandoned him and his group when a panther shrieked at their camp continuously one night. Oddly enough, most native peoples of the Olympic Peninsula did not venture into the interior, because they thought their gods lived there. There are some interesting parallels between some stories of the Himalayan Shangri-La and native legends of a hidden valley in the Olympics, guarded by Skookum....The Chinook jargon does have many different interpretations for the word "Skookum" depending on which expert is consulted. I used MacArthur's 1924 definition, but for me the [Bigfoot] connection was strong once I went to a Skookum place and figure that I stood 10 feet from a smelly Bigfoot on my very first day of looking.

Revisiting the Name Game

Of course, all that has been named on the land and reflected in reports of strange things is not labeled with a sinister moniker such as Spirit, Sacred, or Mystery, which are so obvious. As John Keel, Jim Brandon, and I have noted down through the years, there are other hidden names. Wisconsin researcher Richard Hendricks is like-minded when he writes about the Bray Road Beast: "These spots have statistically more than their fair share of odd sightings or strange events. We note that Jefferson is located near Aztalan, and its many mysteries; Elkhorn, and Bray Road is near Lafayette Township, and the name Lafayette [from Fey, or the faery] appears frequently as a site of paranormal occurrences." Sometimes the name merely sounds like there should be strange things happening at the location, like Chazy, New York, a quiet bedroom and farm community only two miles south of the Canadian Boarder and three miles from Lake Champlain, haunt of the famous lake monster,

Champ. Chazy has a good history of creature accounts, according to Fortean Jim Boyd, highlighted by sightings of giant phantom animals (felines? hyenas?) that attacked and killed local livestock in 1992.

If there is a twilight language to be decoded, if we are observing a ritual working, we should be looking for relevant synchronicities (coincidences that have meaning), which would form a pattern. In acknowledging the possible links between these named locations and Fortean events, the objective is not linear, that is to say, is not solely bound to the immediate and obvious events recorded, but may in fact be a part of a larger, symbolic ritual magnified by the power of the electronic media, for the purpose of processing in the subconscious.

The FBI and the CIA have understood the importance of "twilight language" in many of their investigations. For example, in the Son of Sam murders of New York, the "Wicker" symbolism was deciphered. The British film, *The Wicker Man*, which premiered in the U.S. in 1974 and was screened in New York by a group called Abraxas in April of 1977, during the height of the frenzy of the Son of Sam killings, became pieces of the puzzle. A hit man who participated in both the Son of Sam and Double Initial murders, John Wheat Carr, signed himself, "Wicked King Wicker."

The writings of Michael A. Hoffman II demonstrate other examples. The solving of the Unabom murders involved a certain deeper understanding of the symbols left behind by Theodore Kaczynski. In the Unabom case, the precursor literary work in question has a more prestigious literary pedigree. Joseph Conrad's 1907 book, *The Secret Agent*, concerned a mad professor clothed in rags, who lived in a tiny room where he built a bomb with which he sought to destroy the "idol of science." "Joseph Conrad" was the literary non-de-plume of the Polish writer Theodore Korzeniowski.

In certain murder-suicide, serial, and mass crime rituals a synchronic work of literature, usually fiction, appears before the crimes are perpetrated, serving as a virtual script. In the case of Patty Hearst and the Symbionese Liberation Army (a group which featured salamander symbolism), the book, *Black Abductor*, had been published before the SLA came to the fore, paralleling many incidents that would come to fruition in the activities of Hearst and her comrades. The Oklahoma City bombing had its *Turner Diaries*. The collapse of the Silver Bridge had it Mothman news articles.

Deciphering the symbols is a difficult task, but attuning yourself to looking at the world through special forensic prisms offers surprising results and links. As the CIA knows, "hiding in plain sight" is what this is all about.

Keel has walked this path, talking of assassinations, MIBs, and more, as well. In *The Eighth Tower,* he wrote:

> In my travels I noted a number of odd variations in this name game. Spectacular sightings and landings occurred at places called Misery Bay, Misery Point, Mount Misery, and Misery Hollow. In each case I found the places had been so named because, logically, weird and miserable things had been happening in them for many years—hauntings, murders, strange noises, bizarre phantasms, disappearances of children and animals without explanation. Sightings in Point Pleasant, West Virginia, were followed up by sightings in Point Pleasant, New Jersey. Sometimes UFO sightings or monster appearances will occur simultaneously in two widely scattered places bearing the same name.

My Name Is, My Name Is, My Name Is…Slimey Slim

With great wit, John A. Keel also dealt with the name game associated with people's proper names. His theory for it was very specific:

> The law of synchronicity has created a fascinating statistical anomaly that suggests that witnesses are not accidental but are actually selected. In fact, the deeper you penetrate into this business, the more obvious it becomes that very little chance is involved. The sightings follow preset geographical and time patterns.

And his examples were illuminating:

In 1966–67, people with the surname Reeve(s) were caught up in the UFO games. The members of a Reeves family in Oregon were driven from their home by eerie lights that passed through walls and chased them from room to room like ball lightning (but this was definitely not ball lightning), while larger objects hovered above their roof and shadowy little figures moved about in their fields. A few months before that John Reeves (no relation) of Brooksville, Florida, claimed contact with a being in a space suit who landed on a sand dune. And one of the most prominent UFO investigators of the 1950s and 60s was an engineer named Bryant Reeve.

Mere coincidences, you might say. But ufological lore is shot full of coincidences. One of the [surviving] victims of the collapse of the Silver Bridge in Point Pleasant, West Virginia, site of a big UFO wave in 1967, was named Alvis Maddox. Three months later, in March 1968, a deputy sheriff in Texas was mentioned in a widely published UFO sighting. His name, too, was Alvis Maddox. Some of these coincidences can really boggle the mind.

This reminds me of my exchange with Keel about the name game in 1973, when we were discussing the new reports out of Illinois, from Enfield. On April 25, 1973, Mr. and Mrs. Henry McDaniel returned to their home and Henry had an encounter with a thing that looked like it had three legs, two pink eyes as big as flashlights, and short arms on a four-and-a-half-feet tall and grayish-colored body, along the L&N railroad tracks, in front of his house. I traveled to Enfield, interviewed the witnesses, looked at the siding of the house the Enfield Monster had damaged, heard some strange screeching banshee-like sounds, and walked away bewildered.

John Keel wondered aloud with me about these reports, as he had returned from Point Pleasant well aware of the vortex the McDaniel family had found themselves in. One of the first Mothman witnesses, Linda Scarberry, was, after all, a McDaniel. Her mother saw Mothman. The McDaniel home was the focus of MIBs, telephone troubles, and poltergeist activity, thus involving Parke McDaniel and Mabel McDaniel with the Mothman flap. Keel had uncovered a 1870s story of an individual named McDaniel who had met up with the Devil in New York State's Catskill Mountains. Western Bigfoot Society member Vic McDaniel led expedition members to where he had found a Sasquatch bed in August 1979. As the 20th century ended, Stanley V. McDaniel, a philosophy professor and member of the Society for Planetary SETI Research, began to make a name for himself, to turn a phrase, when he produced *The McDaniel Report*, and a book, *The Case for the Face*, on his research into the possibility of artificial objects on the surface of Mars.

Slimey Slim, Idaho's Payette Lake monster, Fluorescent Freddie, a Bigfoot-type creature seen at French Lick, Indiana, and the Mothman of Point Pleasant, West Virginia, have names too. But it's the names of the witnesses that may tell us more in the final analysis. Additional research and study in this arena is required. It may one day help us predict where flaps might occur ("location, location, location"), when they might occur ("what time is it?), and who might experience it (My name is…).

Those Eyes!

Patrick Huyghe, in *Swamp Gas Times,* tells one of my favorite John Keel stories. During the mid-1980s, there was much interest in UFOs in the Hudson Valley of New York. More than 5,000 individuals, in one of the most populated areas of the U.S., actually saw these things, whatever they were. Huyghe attending a 1987 gathering on the activity, observed: "Some 800 people turned up for the most recent Brewster conference, and everyone knew better than to believe speaker John Keel, author of *UFOs: Operation Trojan Horse,* when he said, 'I'm going to tell you the secret of the flying saucers; then you can all go home.' Everyone laughed. No one went home."

The closer you get, the more you think you see, sometimes the less you know.

Connie Carpenter had one of the best views of the face of

Mothman: "Those eyes! They were very red and once they were fixed on me I couldn't take my own eyes off them." But she could not really describe what she saw, as the eyes were all she truly could remember. "It was horrible, like something out of a science fiction movie."

Those eyes are the metaphor of the whole enigma. We see it but we certainly don't know what we have seen.

Mothman, as an all-encompassing mystery, is in a class by itself. Even if you don't like Keel's theories, you must respect him for his groundbreaking, on-site field work. He didn't go to Point Pleasant thinking he would come away with theories about name games, windows, demon birds, MIBs, and more. While I was writing this book, I talked to Keel more frequently than I have in years. He told me that when he was in Point Pleasant in 1966-1967, he was on the phone almost nightly with his old friend, zoologist Ivan T. Sanderson. Keel asked Sanderson about this bird and that bird to try to place the Mothman sightings into a biological context. Keel carried around drawings of sandhill cranes, herons, and other large birds to show witnesses to discover if these birds were what people were seeing. He came away, instead, with a variety of thoughts and theories that have won him fans, friends, and foes.

Indeed, I find myself still considering possible cryptozoological answers for Mothman, while at the same time appreciating what Keel did. Some of my friends who read this book will think I have gone to the "dark side" by merely allowing myself to think about Mothman, let alone researching Keel and his radical ideas. You see, I am a Fortean, and in a very strange way, Point Pleasant all makes sense to me. Mothman's time has come. Mothman lives. The event wrapped in the riddle called Mothman has focused so many mysteries in one place. We are not able to ignore it, any longer, even if we don't have all the answers yet.

Appendices and Resources

26 "Mothman" Sightings

West Virginia 1966–1967

In 1970, John A. Keel gave a preview of the investigations he had been doing in Point Pleasant in Chapter 18, "West Virginia's 'Mothman'" of his book, *Strange Creatures from Time and Space* (New York: Fawcett, 1970). That book included a table that Keel said contained the 26 "most responsible" sightings of Mothman. Keel has allowed me to reproduce this chart here. It is published below, with the data complete, unedited and unembellished.

Date	Witnesses	Locale	Description
Sept. 1, 1966	Several adults	Scott, Miss.	Man-shaped object maneuvering at low altitude.
Nov. 1, 1966	National Guardsman	Armory, near Camp Conley Rd., Point Pleasant	A large, brown man-shaped figure on limb of tree.
Nov. 12, 1966	5 male adults	Cemetery near Clendenin, W. Va.	A flying, brown human-shaped object.
Nov. 15, 1966	2 married couples	TNT Area, near old power plant, Point Pleasant, W. Va.	Large gray man-shaped creature with blazing red eyes, 10 ft wing span. Pursued witnesses' auto.

Date	Witnesses	Locale	Description
Nov. 16, 1966	3 adults, 3 children	TNT Area, near "igloos"	Tall, grayish creature with glowing red eyes.
Nov. 17, 1966	Teenaged boy	Route 7, near Cheshire, Ohio	Gray man-shaped creature with red eyes and 10 ft wing spread pursued witness' auto.
Nov. 18, 1966	2 firemen	TNT Area	Giant winged creature with red eyes.
Nov. 20, 1966	6 teenagers	Campbells Creek, W.Va.	Gray man-sized creature with red eyes.
Nov. 24, 1966	2 adults, 2 children	Point Pleasant	Giant flying creature with red eyes.
Nov. 25, 1966	Male adult	Highway passing TNT Area	Gray man-like being with red eyes and 10 ft wing spread. Pursued auto.
Nov. 26, 1966	2 male adults, 2 children	Lowell, Ohio	Four giant brown and gray birds, with reddish heads. 5 ft tall, 10 ft wingspans.
Nov. 26, 1966	Housewife	St. Albans, W. Va.	Gray creature with red eyes, taller than a man, standing on lawn.
Nov. 27, 1966	Teenaged girl	Mason, W.Va.	Tall, gray man-shaped being with 10 ft wingspan and red eyes. Pursued auto.
Nov. 27, 1966	2 teenaged girls	St. Albans, W. Va.	Gray seven-foot tall creatures pursued witnesses (who were on foot).

Date	Witnesses	Locale	Description
Dec. 4, 1966	5 pilots	Gallipolis, Ohio, airport.	Giant "bird," appeared to be plane at first. Long neck reported. Estimated speed: 70 mph.
Dec. 6, 1966	Mailman	Maysville, Ky.	Giant birdlike creature in flight.
Dec. 6, 1966	2 adults	TNT Area	Giant gray man-like figure with glowing red eyes.
Dec. 7, 1966	4 adult women	Route 33, Ohio	Brownish-silver man-shaped flying creature with glowing red eyes.
Dec. 8, 1966	2 adult women	Route 35, W.Va.	Shadowy figure on hilltop, two glowing red eyes.
Dec. 11, 1966	1 adult male, 1 boy	TNT Area	Man-shaped figure, gray, flying overhead at great speed.
Dec. 11, 1966	Adult woman	Route 35, W. Va.	Huge gray creature with glowing red eyes, flew past car.
Jan. 11,1967	Housewife	Point Pleasant	Winged being as big as a small plane flew low over Route 62.
Mar. 12, 1967	1 adult woman	Letart Falls, Ohio	Large white flying being with long hair, 10 ft. wingspread, passed directly in front of car.
May 19, 1967	1 adult woman	TNT Area	Flying creature with grow-ing red eyes approached hovering luminous object and disappeared.

Date	Witnesses	Locale	Description
Nov.2. 1967	Adult woman	TNT Area	Giant gray man-like figure gliding swiftly at ground level across field.
Nov. 2, 1967	4 adult males	Chief Cornstalk Park, W. Va.	Witnesses claim to have encountered a giant gray figure with red eyes while hunting. They were so frightened they never thought to raise their rifles.

Windows: Places of High Strangeness within North America

No matter where you live on this planet, someone within two hundred miles of your home has had a direct confrontation with a frightening apparition or inexplicable 'monster' within the last generation. Perhaps it was even your cousin or your next-door neighbor. There is a chance— a very good one—that sometime in the next few years you will actually come face to face with a giant hair-covered humanoid or a little man with bulging eyes, surrounded by a ghostly greenish glow.
—John A. Keel, *Strange Creatures from Time and Space*

There is no money-back guarantee that anyone going to these places will see a spook, will-o-the-wisp, flying saucer, or tumbling geode within the first 10 minutes of arrival. But perhaps there is a certain aura or spirit of place—obviously there is something special about these sites—on which we should concentrate our long-dormant powers of total perception.—Jim Brandon, *Weird America*

Geographical 'devil names' worldwide may indicate, as they seem to in America, locales high in Fortean energy and strangeness. These places deserve some extra attention, for from the stray sod to the fairy ring, from the haunted glen to the Devil's Den, there lies many a riddle to unfold.
—Loren Coleman, *Mysterious America*

John A. Keel coined the term "window" and the concept of the "window area" to denote a special spot of concentrated unexplained activity. This localized furor can take the form of monster sightings, UFO reports, MIB encounters, poltergeist accounts, and haunted high jinks. The following list reflects examples of bedeviled areas, spook light locations, railroad ghost light places, and haunted locales, which may be called "windows." It contains, as well, very specifically focused sites that may be smaller, defined zones within the window areas, literally spooky spots. Paying attention to this list will enhance awareness, but, needless to say, windows shift and new ones open all the time. And don't forget to check out your local grassy knolls, baldknobs, and counties with names based on "Devil," "Hockomock," and "LaFayette"!

UNITED STATES OF AMERICA

Alabama
Battles Wharf
Birmingham: Bayview Bridge
Cahaba: Salt Marsh Hall
Courtland: Rocky Hill Castle
Demopolis: Gainesville
Furman: Savage Hill
Kinston: Harriet Cemetery
Marion: Carlisle Hall
Mobile
  Bienville Square
  Madison Manor
  Toulmin House
Montgomery: Pratt Hall/Huntington College
Pratville: Gurney Manufacturing Factory
Prichard: Bliunt High School
Selma: Sturdivant Hall
Tuscaloosa
  Old Drish Plantation Home
  Smith Hall Museum, University of Alabama
Vernon: Local road

Alaska
Lake Iliamna: Mountains
Sitka: Baranof Castle

Arizona
Cerbat Mountains
Douglas: Gadsden Hotel
Kingman: Death Trap Mountains
Phoenix: Indian School Road
Superstition Mountains
Tinajas Atlas Spring: Laguna Prieta and Mission of the Four Evangelists
Tucson
  Old Cerro Colorado Mine
  Stone Avenue Underpass
Wilcox: Alkali Flats

Arkansas
Arkadelphia: Barkman House
Clarksville: College of the Ozarks
Crossett: Missouri-Pacific Railroad
Fayetteville: Lake Wedington
Fort Smith
  Jailhouse

Rector Heights
Gordon: Missouri-Pacific Railroad
Helena: 404 College Street
Ozark Mountains
Pine Bluffs: Sawdust Bridge
Tucker: Prison Farm

California
Aetna Springs: Resort
Alabama Hills
Bel-Air: Pink (Mansfield) House
Berkeley
   Faculty Club
   Siegal Rock
Beverly Hills
   Elke Sommer's Benedict Canyon
Home
   2320 Bowman Drive
Big Bear City: Rebel Ridge
Bodega: Charlene's Yesterday
Museum
Bodie: Graveyard
Breckenridge Mountains
Bridgeport: Poor Farm
Camarillo: State Hospital
Chino
Clayton
   Ingram Cave
   Live Oak Cemetery
   Morgan Territory Road
   Town Hall
Cobblestone Mountain
Coloma: Vineyard House
Coulterville: Highway 32
Fair Oaks: American River/Sailor's
Bar
Fountain Valley: Stowe House
Fresno
   1818 Tyler Street
   St. John's Cathedral
Funeral Mountains
Gardena: Airport

Georgetown: Elliott Home
Green Lake
Hillsborough: 85 Country Club Drive
Hollywood: Houdini Mansion
grounds
Irvine Beach: Peters Canyon Road
Julian: Oriflamme Mountains
Kelso Valley: Sheep Springs
Kennedy Meadow: Nine Mile Canyon
Laguna Beach: Hangover House
Lake Tahoe
Little Lake
Los Angeles
   Ardmore Blvd
   City Hall
   Eagle Rock
   Hillcrest Church
   96th Street
   Petit Street
   337 S. Main Street
   Valentino's Movie Studio
Lynwood: Lago Avenue
Mare Island: Naval Reserve
Mill Valley: Tiburon Point Castle
Misery Mountain
Monterey: Casa Bodega Liquor Store
Monterey: Robert Lewis Stevenson's
Houston Street House
Mount Shasta
Mount Tamalpais
North Hollywood: Riverside Drive
Oakland Hills: Slaughter Hunting
Lodge
Oakland: 1904 Franklin Street
Ojai: Creek Road
Orange County
   Black Star Canyon/Irvine Mansion
   El Toro Cemetery
   Knott's Berry Farm
   Mission San Juan Capistrano
   Peters Canyon
   Santa Ana Canyon

Silverado Canyon
Trabuco Creek
Yorba Linda Cemetery
Palo Alto: 500 Block Emerson Street
Pigeon Point: Coast Guard Lighthouse
Pomona: Casa Alvarado
Sacramento: 5848 14th Avenue
Saint Helena: Spring Hill Farm
San Diego
  Navy Electronic Lab/Loma Portal
  Whaley House
San Francisco
  Alcatraz
  Bank of America
  Bush and Octavia Street
  *California Street near Fairmont
Hotel*
  Lombard Street
  Russian Hill
  Sutro Baths
  Toravel Street
  2544 Clement Avenue
  2221 Washington Street
San Jose
  LeBaron Hotel/Room 538
  Sarah Winchester Mystery House
San Simeon: Hearst Castle
Santa Cruz Mountains
Smith Valley
Sonoma
  Blue Wing Inn
  Wolf House
Stockton: Rose Street
Sunnyvale: Toys-R-Us Store
Tehachapi Mountains
Thousand Oaks
  Missionary Baptist Church
  Stagecoach Inn
Tustin: Pacific Street
Valley of the Moon
Ventura
  Meta Street

Mission San Buenaventura
Ventura Theater
Wheeler Canyon
Yerba Buena Island: Lighthouse
Yucaipa: 33843 Fairview Road

Colorado
Arena Creek
Deadman Creek
Denver
  Bradmar House
  4100 S. University Avenue
  2334 Lawrence Street
Dory Hill
Greeley: Poudre River
Hall Valley
Jamestown: Quartz Mine
Marshall Pass: Union Pacific Railroad
Pike's Peak
Silver Cliff: Cemetery
Westminster: Andrews House

Connecticut
Bridgeport: Lindley Street
Cornwall
  Dark Entry Ravine
  Dudleytown
East Hartford: Hockcanum Caseway
Greenwhich: St. Paul's Episcopal
Church
Groton Long Point
Hanging Hills
Milldale: West Peak
Moodus: Mount Tom
Mount Riga
New Haven: Woolsley Hall, Yale
University
North Woodstock: Brickyard Road
Norwich: Spite House
Stratford: Phelps House
Talcott Mountains
West Hartford: Reservoir

Windham: Frog Pond

Delaware
Brandywine: Riverview Cemetery
Dover
  King George III Inn
  Woodburn (Governor's) Mansion
Newark: Brookside

District of Columbia
Capitol Building
Decatur House
Ford's Theater
Fort McNair
Halcyon House
Lincoln Memorial
National Theater
Navy Yard
Octagon
Pentagon
Petersen House
Tingey House
White House
Woodrow Wilson House

Florida
Bartow: Railroad
Cayo Pelau
Coral Gables: Miami Biltmore Hotel
Defuniak Springs: Eden State Garden
Fort George Island: Kingsley
Plantation
Key West: Audubon House
Miami
  Laubheim Warehouse
  Tropication Arts
  22nd Avenue and 28th Street
Oklawaha: Bradford House
Oviedo: State Road 13
Tallahassee: Department of
Corrections Building
Wakulla Springs

West Palm Beach: La Petite Poodle
Winter Springs: Turner Home

Georgia
Adel: No Man's Friend Pond
Atlanta
  Fort McPherson
  Oakland Cemetery
  St. Michael's Church
Columbus: Springer Opera House
Dale: Telegraph Tower
Kinchafoonee Creek
Macon: Railroad
McDonough: Railroad
Oakville: Old Washingham House
Plains: Old Carter House
Riverside: Fort Benning
Saint Simon's Island
  Christ Church
  Ebo Landing
Whitmire Hill

Hawaii
Ewa: 91-1668 Pahiki Street
Honolulu: Hawaiian Village Hilton
Kawela Bay
Kohala Mountains
Mauna Loa: Ka-upe
Nuuana Valley
Old Waimea: Firehouse
Parker Ranch
Waiane: 85-904 Imipono Street

Idaho
McCammon: I-15, between mileposts
47 and 57

Illinois
Alsip: Cemetery at 115th Street
Bartonville: State Hospital Cemetery
Belleville: Main and 17th Street
Chicago

Biograph Theater
Clark Street near Lincoln Park
Holy Family Church
Hull House
Hyde Park
Irish Castle
Kaiser Hall
Kedzie Avenue
Knights of Columbus at 33rd Street
St. Rita's Church
3375 Oakley Avenue
Crestwood: Bachelor Grove Cemetery
Cumberland County: Embarrass River
Decatur: Stevens Creek
Edwardsville: R.C. Scheffel and
Company
Equality: Old Slave House
Jonesboro: Dug Hill
Justice: Resurrection Cemetery
Lawrenceville: High School
Macomb: Charles Willey Farm
Mason: Little Wabash River Bridge
McLeansboro: Lakey's Creek
Oak Lawn: Holy Sepulchre Cemetery
Oakley: Peck Cemetery
Springfield
Lincoln Home
  Oak Ridge Cemetery
  Old Courthouse
Tunnel Hill: Skunk Hollow
Urbana
  Urbana High School tower
  Woodlawn Cemetery
  Ursa: Old Covered Bridge
  Voorhies: Voorhies Castle
  Woodstock: Opera House

Indiana
Benton: Rising Sun Cemetery
Danville: Railroad Bridge/White Lick
Creek
Decatur County: Sand Creek

Dublin: Cry Woman Bridge
Indianapolis
  Hannah House
  2910 West Delaware Street
Lafayette
Lake Manitou
Notre Dame: Washington Hall
Osceola: Greenlawn Avenue

Iowa
Columbus Junction
Davenport: Pi Kappa Chi Fraternity
Dubuque: Ham House
Iowa City: Sumter House
Millville: Split-Level Road
Mount Pleasant
St. Mary's: Farm
Spirit Canyon

Kansas
Clay County: Jesse James Homestead
Doniphan: Doniphan Lake
Edwardsville: Kansas Pacific Railroad
Fort Riley: George Custer House
Lawrence: Old Delaware Mills
Manhattan: Manhattan Avenue
Oak Canyon
Sterling: Broadway Station

Kentucky
Bardstown: Nelson County Jail
Blue Mountains
Brandenburg: Woodland
Dunnville: Old Bailey House
Frankfort: Liberty Hall
Louisville
  Camp Taylor
  Fern Creek
  Stuckenberg Place
Mulberry Hill
Owensboro: Wilson's Ferry
Pikeville: Chloe Creek Mine

Woolrich
Burnt Hill
Hockomock Point

Maryland
Annapolis
Chandler Mansion
42 East Street
West Point
Baltimore
Fayette Street Westminster
Presbyterian Churchyard
1448 Meridene Drive
Hampton Mansion
Locust Point
USF Constellation
Boonesboro: South Mountain
Church Creek
Clinton: Surrat Tavern
Crisfield
Asbury Church Cemetery
Horsey Place
Emmitsburg: Cemetery
Fort Howard: Todd House
Golden Hill: Catholic Church
Gum Briar Swamp
Hebron
Indian Head
Oyster Point
Port Tobacco: Rose Hill
Smith Island
Towson: Hampton National Historic
Site
Warfieldburg: Ore Mine Bridge
Westminster
Leigh Master Estate
Maryland Hunt Cup Course

Massachusetts
Amesbury: Barrow Hill
Ashland: John Stone's Inn
Atholl

Crescent Street Bridge
Sanders Street
Silver Lake
Barnstable: Public Housing Authority
Bish-Bash Falls State Park: Bish-Bash
Falls
Boston
1 Arlington Street
1 Garrett Street
Boston Harbor Islands
Apple Island
Clark's Island
George's Island: Fort Warren
Long Island
Cedar Grove Cemetery
King's Lane
Logan Airport
Bridgwater: Hockomock Swamp
Cambridge
The Commons
Riedesel Mansion
Charlton: Massachusetts Turnpike
Information Center
Cohasset: Ship's Chandlery
Danvers: Gallows Hills
Dighton: Colonel Richmond House
Douglas: Orchard
Dover: Polka Rock
Great Berrington: Three Mile Hill
Hadley
Elm Valley
Huntington House
Wilder Hall, Mount Holyoke College
Halifax: Davis Farm
Haverhill: Buttonwoods Museum
Hingham: Eastgate Lane
Hopkinton: 86 Elm Street
Ipswich: Congregational Church
Lake Quannapowette
Lawrence: 26 Florence Street
Lowell: Christian Hill
Lynn: Lynn Woods

Reservation/Dungeon Rock
Malden: Cemetery
Marblehead
  Oakum Bay
  Screeching Lady Beach
Marshfield: Phillips Mansion
Medford: Rock Hill Estate
Medway: Dinglehole
Methuen: 1 Linton Avenue
Milton: Milton Hill
Newburyport: 32 Charles Street
North Adams: Hoosac Tunnel
Pittsfield: Pittsfield and North Adams
Railroad
Plum Island
Quincy: St. Mary's Cemetery
Salem: Joshua Ward House
Somerville: Washington Street
Springfield
  Hotel
  7 Butler Street
Warren: Waternomee Falls
Wellesley: Golf Course
Woburn
  Black House
  Central House
  Dunham's Pond
  First Baptist Church
  Horn Pond
  Wright's Pond

Michigan
Caribou Island
Detroit
  5508 Martin Street
  Howard and 19th Street
  Nain Rouge
Dixboro
Frankfort: LaRue Home
Grand Rapids
  Prospect Avenue SE
  Sanford Mansion

Grand Sable Banks
Grosse Point Park
Hamtramck: 9485 Mitchell Street
Holland: Lodge Post
Holly: Robinson Home
Lansing: St. Joseph Cemetery
Lapeer: Calhoun Street
McBain: McBain House
Munising: West Superior Street
Stambaugh: Riverton Mine
Westland: Butler Cemetery

Minnesota
Baudette: Railroad
Canby
Collegeville: St. John's Abbey
Crookston
Eagle Lake
Gibbon
Hasings
Lake Park
Minneapolis
  Chelberg House
  City Hall
  Guthrie Theater
Owatonna
Russell
St. Paul
  Forepaugh's
  476 Summit Avenue
  Grigg's House
Silver Lake
Vondell Brooks

Missisippi
Artesia: Railroad track
Beauregard: E.A. Rowan House
Gulfport: Cahill House
Natchez
  Cottage Gardens
  Glenburnie House
  King's Tavern

Longwood Plantation
Raliegh: Town Cemetery
Sumner: Boone Jerkins House
Tupelo: Natchez Trace Parkway/Witch
Dance

Missouri
Back Creek: Highway 61
Bolvair: Highway 13
Breadtray Mountain
Cape Girardeau: Lorimer Cemetery
Cassville: Moaning Mountain
Eldorado Springs
Everton: Old Payne Orchard
Fayette: Lilac Hill
Flat River: Red Onion Cave
Galena: Old McCord Farm
Hannibal: Bear Creek Cemetery
Joplin: 12 miles SW
Kansas City: Emerson House,
University of Missouri
Laddonia: Harbison Dairy Farm
Lake of the Ozarks: Glaize Park
Louisiana: River Road
Matthews: Cotton Belt Railroad
Reeds Springs: Ghost Pond
Saint Genevieve: 1 North Street
Saint Joseph: Pacific House
Saint Louis
  Calvary Drive
  Clarion Hotel
Webster Groves
White River: Highway 13

Montana
Butte: Orphan Girl Mine
Missoula: South Fifth Street

Nebraska
Blackbird Hill
Lincoln: White Building, Nebraska
Wesleyan University

Norfolk
  110 Michigan
  125 E. Park
Omaha: Court House

Nevada
Black Rock Range
Oregon Canyon
Virginia City: Mary Louise Hospital

New Hampshire
Appledore Island: Babb's Cove
Chelsea: Orange County Jail
Derry: Beaver Lake
Hampton: Moulton House
Henniker: Ocean-Born Mary House
Isles of Shoals
Lancaster: Farrar House
Pittsfield: Ehrhardt Home
Sawyer's River
Troy
White Island
Woodsville: Lumber Mill

New Jersey
Atlantic City: Fire Engine Company
No. 3
Barnegat Bay
Camden: 522 North Fifth Street
Cranbury: Truxton House
Flanders: Central Railroad of NJ
Jersey City: Wild Goose Tavern
Keansburg: St. Ann's Catholic Church
Lake Wanaque: Hills
Long Valley: High Bridge Railroad
Mickleton: Bodo Otto House
Middletown: Spy House
Montclair: Rooming House
Morristown: Wedgewood Inn
Mount Holly
  Fair Haven
  Foy Homestead

Pompton Lakes: Sunnybank
Saddle River: Ringwood Manor
Schooley's Mountain
Scotch Plains
Shark River: Money Hill
Vincetown: Granite Castle
Winfield: 2-C Wavecrest Avenue

New Mexico
Alamogordo: 1712 Van Court
Carlsbad: Pecos River/Seep Canyon
Llano: River
Prewitt: Apache Burial Grounds
Taos: Dennis Hopper Hacienda

New York
Albany
  Graceland Cemetery
  NY Central Railroad
  Parsonage
Berne: Simmons Factory
Biddle Hollow
Binghamton: Vestal Home
Boytonville: State Route 1
Cherry Valley: Old Randall Place
Cincinnatus: Chenango Quarry
Cooperstown: River Street
Cortland: Joe Charles Sport Shop
Croton-On-Hudson: Van Cortlandt
Manor House
Dosoris Island
Dunderberg
East Northport: 3 Purdy Avenue
Fort Johnson
Fredonia: State University College
Building
Glen Cove: Morgan Hall
Greenwich: St. Paul's Episcopal
Rectory
Hydesville: Fox Homestead
Irvington: Ardsley-On-Hudson
Kinderhook: Lindenwald

Livingston: Widow Mary's Place
Long Island: Mount Misery
Mamaroneck: Seven Oaks
Mohawk: Gelston Castle
Mount Van Hoevenberg
New York City
  Atlantic Bridge
  Austen House
  Bayswater Road
  Bergen House
  Cafe Bizarre
  Central Park
  Church of St. Bartholomew
  Clinton Court
  Conference House
  Crawley House
  Dakota Apartments
  Division Avenue
  8th Avenue
  84 Gurnsey Street
  Ellis Island
  11 Bank Street
  Empire Theater
  51 West 10th Street
  52 Willoughby Street
  471 Central Park West
  44th Street and 9th Avenue
  Henderson Avenue
  Hotel des Artistes
  Howard Beach
  John Jay House
  Metropolitan Opera
  Morris-Jumel Mansion
  Old Merchant's House
  Park Avenue
  Riverside Drive
  Rodenberg House
  Roosevelt Avenue Station
  1780 House/Stamford Hill
  St. Mark's-in-the-Bowery Church
  Schubert Alley
  Snyder Avenue

1096 Lafayette Avenue
10th Street
34th Street and 3rd Avenue
Tillary and Concord Street
12 Gay Street
21st Street
27 Jane Street
226 West Fifth Avenue
West 87th Street
West 57th Street
West 56th Street
West 45th Street
West 12th Street
Women's Detention Prison
Nine Cornered Lake
Onondaga: Moor
Oswego: Fort Ontario
Pitcher Springs: Crofton
Campsite/Otselic Valley
Poughkeepsie: Christ Church Rectory
Ramapo River
Rochester: Hawley Street
Rye
  Barberry Lane
  The Cedars
Sackets Harbor: Samuel Guthrie
Home
Sag Harbor
Salem: Schoolhouse
Schenectady: Ellis Hospital Elevator
B-1
Seaford: 1648 Redwood Path
Shelter Island
South Gilboa: Spook Woods
Syracuse: Syracuse Area Landmark
Theater
Tarrytown: Van Alen House
Ticonderoga: Fort Ticonderoga
Waterford: St. Mary's Church
Watkins Glen State Park
Wellsville: Pink House

West Point: Military Academy, Room
4714
Woodstock
Youngstown: Old Fort Niagara

North Carolina
Ashboro: Morrow Mountain
Asheville
  Royal Mountain
  Starnes Avenue
Balsam Mountains
Big Laural
Burke County: Brown
Mountains/Catawba Valley
Cape Fear River
Chapel Hill: Louisville and Nashville
Railroad
Charlotte
  Great Gray Barn
  South Park Shopping Center
Cleveland County: Kadesh Church
Dallas: Old Jail House
Dunn: 809 E. Harnett
Eldorado: Old Coggins Gold Mine
Epsom: Neal Farm
Fayetteville: A.S. Slocumb House
French Broad River
Grandfather Mountain: Sawmill
Green Hill: Haunted Hollow
Havelock: S.A. Long Plantation
Hillsbourgh
  Haw Place
  Seven Hearths
Knotts Island
Lincoln County: Engleside Mansion
Maco: Atlantic Coast Line Railroad
Trestle/Hood's Creek
McAdenville: Adams Springs House
Raleigh
  Governor's Mansion
  Holman House
  Poole's Woods

Roanoke Island
Rockford: Burris House
Rutherfordton: Jailhouse
Salola Mountain
Silver City: Harper Cross Roads
Statesville: Atlantic Coast Line
Railroad
Thomasville: San-Mor Inc. Factory
Troy: Sut Creek Bridge
Warsaw: Atlantic Coast Line Railroad
White Oak: Old Roberson Place
Willow Creek
Wilmington: Price-Gause House
Winston-Salem
Brothers House
Salem Tavern

North Dakota
Fargo: Road to Kindred
Powers Lake
Richardson: Wild Plum School

Ohio
Belmont: Woods School
Bethlehem: Woodside Pet Cemetery
Blendon: 3670 Karikal Drive
Blue Ash: Hazelwood
Bowling Green: University
Apartments
Cincinnati
1020 West 8th Street
Cleveland
1115 Leading Avenue
4207 Mason Court SE
Franklin Castle
Dayton: 354 Forrest Avenue
Fayette County: Cherry Hill
Findlay: Town Cemetery
Galion: 937 Harding Avenue
Gallipolis: Deluse Farmhouse
Granville: Buxton Inn
Johnson's Island

Kent: Van Campen Hall, Kent State
University
Lake Hope: Hope Furnace
Pickaway County: Timmon's Bridge
Pleasant Valley
Shelby: Yazoo and Mississippi Valley
Railroad
Somerset: Otterbein Cemetery
Waterloo: Columbian House

Oklahoma
Bristow: Jailhouse
Kiamichi Mountains
Oklahoma City: Biltmore Hotel
Sand Springs
Tulsa: Berryhill
Vinita: Circle J Ranch

Oregon
Ashland: 35 S. 2nd Street
Clackamus County: Old Campbell
Land Claim
Clatsop Spit
Copper: Rouge River Campground
Eugene: Bornholz House
Portland
546 Marshall Street
Park Avenue
The Dalles: McNutt Hom
Weston: Road

Pennsylvania
Altoona
Baker Mansion
Rosella Rock
Blue Mountains: Mission House
Braddock: Thomson Works
Cheltenham: East Cheltenham Free
Library
Conewago Creek: Conewago Creek
Bridge
Coudersport

Black Forest
Cherry Springs Hotel Site
Cross Fork: Gravel Lick Trail
Fairfield
  Furnace Road
  Rombin's Nest Shop
  Fishing Creek
Germantown: Loudon Mansion
Gettysburg
  Battlefield
  Lutheran Church
  Tavern
Hammersley Park
  Hotel
  Twin Sisters
Hanover: Pigeon Hills
Harrisburg: Den Baron Farm
Honesdale: Bethany Colony Mansion
Indiana: Watt's Hill
Lafayette Hill
Levittown: Bolton Mansion
Littlestown: Route 194 Bridge
Mahoning: 1161 North Liberty Street
McKeesport: 1515 Evans Avenue
McSherrystown: Conewago Roman
Catholic Chapel
Millvale: Croatian Catholic Church
New Castle: Broad Mountain
Oleona: Ole Bull Castle
Philadelphia
  Bouvier Street
  Chalkley Hill
  South Fifth Street
  Stockton House
  Walnut and 5th Street
Pittsburgh
  Broad Street Tabernacle Church
  1129 Ridge Avenue
  Hawthorne Street
  KDKA-TV Station
  Lincoln Avenue
  Montview Place

1724 Harcor Drive
Port Allegany: Two Mile Run
Prospectville: Graeme Park
Smethport: McKean County Jail
Valley Forge State Park
York: Center Square

Rhode Island
Barrington: Baron Farm
Block Island
Foster: Ramtail Factory
Hopkins Hill: Witch Rock
Johnston: 40 Pocasset Street
Mount Tom
Narragansett: Wedderburn House
North Kingston: Swamptown
Providence: Martin Road
Quonset: Route One

South Carolina
Bamberg: U.S. 301
Bush River
Camden
  Court Inn
  116 Mill Street
Charleston
  Belvidere Mansion
  Fenwick Hall
  59 Church Street
  Old Goose Creek Plantation
  St. Phillip's Church
Dorchester County: Sheep Island
Road
Edisto Island
Gaston: Poor Hope Plantation
Georgetown: Litchfield Plantation
Goshen Hill: Goshen Hill Road
McClellanville: Hampton
Pawley's Island
Spartanburg: Foster's Tavern

South Dakota
Deadwood
Ellsworth Air Force Base

Tennessee
Adams: Bell Caves
Bolivar: Wedding Cake House
Charleston: Coon Hunters
Headquarters Building
Chickamauga: Chickamauga National
Military Park.
Clarksville: Oaklands
Farmington: Hollond House
Gordonsburg: Natchez Trace
Parkway/Lewis Monument
Kingston: Pastorium
Memphis
  Graceland Mansion
  9169 Tulane Road
  Orpheum Theater
  Woodruff Mansion
Mountain City: Fiddler's Rock
Murfreesboro: Stones River
Battlefield national Park
Nashville: 1627 9th Avenue
Shelbyville: 610 North Jefferson
Street
Shiloh: Shiloh Battlefield/Cherry
Mansion
Snow Creek: Crazy Horse Hollow
Sparta: Milksick Mountain
Surgoinsville: Old White Oak
Taylor's Community: Austin Farm

Texas
Austin
  Governor's Mansion
  School for the Blind
Big Thicket
Brazos River: Bailey Plantation
Brownsville
  Community Development

Corporation Office
  Olive Electric Inc. Office
Chinati Mountains
Chisholm Hollow
Chisos Mountains
Cisco: Old B.Y. Woodson Place
Dallas
  Banner Mansion
  Dealey Plaza
  Prairie Avenue
  White Rock Lake
El Paso: Trans Mountain Road/Cotton
Wood Springs
Galveston: Mott House
Goliad: La Bahalia Mission
Henderson: Old Howard Homestead
Houston
  1110 Edwards Street
  1425 W. Gray Street
  NASA Space Center area
  106 E. Alber Street
  Public Library
  7224 Kernel Street
LaPorte: Lafitte House
Laredo: Laredo Independent School
District's Azios Building
Llano: Ranch House
Lufkin: Southern Pacific Railroad
Marfa: Southern Pacific Railroad
San Antonio: Brooks House
San Marcos: Bridge
San Patricio: Nueces River
Saratoga: Bragg Road
Sulphur Springs: Negro Hollow
Waller County: Liendo Plantation

Utah
Salt Lake City
  Bailey Seed Company
  Cook Home

Vermont
Albany: Old Hayden Mansion
Chittenden
  Honto's Cave
  Old Eddy Homestead
Essex Junction: Central Vermont
Railroad
Mt. Glastenbury
Waterford Township: Washburn Barn

Virginia
Abington: Martha Washington Inn
Alexandria
  Lee Mansion
  Ramsey House
Amelia: Haw Branch Plantation
Beaverdam: Scotchtown
Belle Haven
Bowling Green: Old Mansion
Buck Hills Caves
Cedar Creek
Charles City
  Shirley Plantation
  Westover Mansion
Charlottesville
  Carrsgrove
  Castle Hill
  Michie Tavern
  Monticello
  The Farm
Fork Union: Careby Hall
Fredericksberg
  Chatham/Lacy House
  Fall Hill Plantation
  Federal Hill
  Kenmore
Gloucester County
  Paynton Hall
  Rosewell
Hampton: Fort Monroe
Hanover: Barksdale Theater
Linden: Pecatone

Loudon County: Noland House
Luray: Corry House
Mathews: Old House Woods
Middletown: Belle Grove Plantation
Smoke House
Norfolk
  City Park
  Norfolk Museum
  Robin Hood Apartments
Old Rag Mountain: Pheasant Hill
Petersburg: Centre Hill Mansion
Port Royal: Elmwood Plantation
Portsmouth
  Chickahominy River
  London Street and Canal Street
  949 Florida Avenue
Richmond
  Bacon's Castle/Old Lawne Creek
  Church Graveyard
  Ninth Street
Stafford: Aquia Church graveyard
Staunton: Dudley Place
Suffolk: Old Jackson and Whaleyville
Railroad Bed/Jackson Road
Virginia Beach
  Chesapeake Beach and Rescue Station
  Witch Duck Point
Williamsburg
  Edgewood Inn
  Governor's Palace
  Wyth House

Washington
Bald Mountain
Eagle Gorge: Burlington Northern
Railroad
Grass Mountain
Ilwaco: Beard's Hall
Seattle
  Boylston Street
  905 E. Pine Street

Spokane: Monaghan Hall/Gonzaga
University

West Virginia
Fayette County: Mount Carbon
Flatwoods
Knob Fork
Little Sewell Mountain
Mill Creek
Monogah: Number Six Mine
Moorefield: Cole Mountain
Moundsville
Point Pleasant
  *Chief Cornstalk Public Hunting
    Area*
  TNT Area
  Old Silver Bridge site
Ravenswood: Movie Theater
Rich Mountain
Ripley: Ghost Ridge
Sumnersville: Peter Creek Valley
Valley Bend
Wetzel County: Rock Camp

Wisconsin
Burke Township: Ghost Hill
Delafield: Rosslynne Manse
Eagle River: Old Railroad Bed/Dog
Meadow
Elkhorn: Bray Road
Evansville: East Side Steak House
Fremont: Old Gottlieb Farm
Germantown: Old Buth Farm
Hale's Corners: Layton House Inn
Grounds
Hudson: Coulee Road
Lake Milles: Rock Lake
Madeline: Ojibway Burial Grounds
Madison
  County Jail
  Noe Woods
  Seminole Highway

Merrill: Scott Mansion
Merrimac: Ferry House Inn
Milwaukee
  Bading House
  Giddings Boarding House
  Grand Avenue
  Hobart House
  Palmer's Addition
Mineral Point: Old Military Ridge
Road
Mount Horeb: Knut K. Lunde Home
Oak Hill: Pumpkin Hollow
Omro: Fox River Bridge
Oneida Lake: Indian Burial Grounds
Oshkosh: Paine Art Center
Pewaukee: Octagon House
Platteville: Negro Head
Poy Sippi
Prescott: Walnut Street
Ridgeway
  Cemetery
  Messerschmidt Hotel Grounds
  Military Ridge Road
  Petra Homestead
River Falls: Colonel Charles Parker
Mansion
Shawano: Old Kopelkie Farm
Verona: Route 1
Waukesha: Ravensholme
West Algoma: Town Street
Wisconsin Dells
  Dell House
  Elephant Rock

Wyoming
Telephone Canyon

CANADA

Alberta
Daysland
Frog Lake

British Colombia
Arrow Lakes
Chilliwack: 342 Williams Street North
Fraser River: Mile 81
Morris Valley
Oak Bay
Vancouver
  Race Rocks/Zone of Silence
  West 11th Street
Victoria: City Park/2668 Uplands

Labrador
Chibongamon Lake

Manitoba
Portage la Prairie: Indian Burial
Grounds
Winnipeg
  McVicar Block
  Mother Tucker's Restaurant
  St. Andrew's
  St. John's Cathedral
Woodridge: Forest

New Brunswick
Fredericton: Christ Church Cathedral
French Fort Cove
Grand Manan
  Big Wood Island
  Cheney's Island
  Kent Island
Howe's Lake: Hangman's Hill
Keenebecasis: Ryan's Castle
Lincoln: Glasier Mansion
Lorneville: Ghost Rock
Mispec: Ghost Hollow

Moncton: Reinsborough Place
Newcastle: Dungarvon River
Restigouche River
Rexton: Richibucto-Rexton Road
Saint John: Hazen Castle Site
Saint John River: Paddy Hollow
Camp

Newfoundland
Conche
Port-au-Coix

Nova Scotia
Amherst
  Cox Cottage
  Princess and Church Street
Caledonia Mills: McDonald
Homestead
Cape Breton/Barrachois: Nova Scotia
Railroad
Eastern Passage: Devil's Island
Halifax: Citadel Hill
Mineville
Sable Island
Springhill
White Head Island: Lighthouse
Yarmouth: Vengeance

Ontario
Algonquin Provincial Park
Belleville
  Home for Orphaned Children
  Ticonderoga Reserve
Black Lake
Brantford: St. Luke's Anglican Church
Brockville: Alban's Point
Cherry Valley
Etobicoke: Prince Edward Drive
Guelph: Rexdale
Hamilton: Brucedale Drive
Indian River
Kingston: Old Aykroyd Place

Lindsay: 33 Cambridge Street South
London: Colborne Street
Manitoulin Island
Milton: Harland Road
Mississauga: Cooksville
Moose River
Nipissing: Waterfalls Lodge
North London: McGhee Place
Peterborough: Bon Echo
Picton: Queen Street
Saint Catherine's: Garden City Dry
Cleaners
Saint Thomas: Alma College
Scarborough: Lawrence Avenue East
Six Nations Reserve
South Bay: Mariner's Cemetery
Streetsville: Mississauga Road and
Steeles Avenue
Sudbury: Highway 17
Thorah Island
Thornhill: Annswell
Toronto
  Ardmore Road
  Bagot Court
  Bay Street
  Bleeker Street
  Chisholm Avenue
  Colborne Lodge
  College Street
  Duke at Sherbourne Street
  Dundas Street
  Dunfield Street
  82 Bond Street
  Grand Opera House
  Hillholme Road
  Humber River
  Jarvis Street
  Mackenzie Hall
  Old City Hall
  174 Avenue Road
  Queen Street West
  Silverwood Avenue

  Sumach Street
  Sunnyside
  University College
  Walmer Road
  Wellesley Street
  Yorkville
Wallaceburg: Belledoon
Windsor: Old Crandall Home

Prince Edward Island
Charlottetown: Binstead
Holland Cove

Quebec
Acton Vale: Saint-Onge Home
Charlesbourg: Chateau Bigot
Hudson: Hudson Hotel
Ile Dupes: Church
Ile-aux-Coudres: Seal Rocks
Montreal
  Hotel-Dieu
  Queen Elizabeth Hotel
  St. Sauvener
  Sainte Famille Street
Quebec City: Notre-Dame-de-Grace
Richmond Gulf

Saskatchewan
Kindersley
Moose Mountain

Mothman Bibliography and Other Resources

Scores of books and articles have been written on anomalous winged creatures, big birds, thunderbirds, giant bats, phantom avian entities, and flying humanoids. This bibliography does not attempt to capture the entire literature on these creatures, but endeavors to bring together in one bibliography all of the major works published on Mothman and the 1966-1967 events occurring during the flap at Point Pleasant, West Virginia. John A. Keel's works reflect the initial and most complete chronicling of these incidents. His firsthand accounts and theorizing have produced other Mothman information in various publications, which may not initially appear to be specific to Mothman. This bibliography contains a complete publishing record of all editions of John A. Keel's *The Mothman Prophecies*. Titles noted under one author are listed chronologically, by publishing history, not alphabetically. Except where indicated, all citations denote an alleged nonfiction work.

Barker, Gray. *The Silver Bridge.* Clarksburg, WV: Saucerian Books, 1970 (novel).

Beckley, Timothy Green. "Red-Eyed Winged Creature Terrorizes West Virginia Town." *Beyond 2.* May 1969, pp. 106–16.

Chorvinsky, Mark. "Cryptozoo Conversation with John A. Keel." *Strange Magazine.* 5, 1990, pp. 35–40.

Clark, Jerome. "Mothman." *Encyclopedia of Strange and Unexplained Physical Phenomena.* Detroit: Gale, 1993, pp. 228–231.

—— "Keel, John Alva." *The UFO Encyclopedia 2nd Edition: The Phenomenon from the Beginning, Volume 1.* Detroit: Omnigraphics, 1998, pp. 550–552.

Clark, Jerome, and Loren Coleman. *Creatures of the Outer Edge.* New York: Warner, 1978.

Coleman, Loren. "Big Birds, Bighoot." *Fate*, July 1999, pp. 15–16.

—— "Mysterious World: Mothman." *Fate*, July 1999, pp. 14–16.

Downes, Jonathan. *The Owlman and Others.* Exeter, UK: CFZ Publications, 1997.

Ecker, Don. "Q & A: Author John Keel: A Godfather's Tour of the UFO 'Borderland'." *UFO* 4,4, September/October 1989, pp. 30–35.

Farish, Lucius. "On Maintaining an Even Keel." *Caveat Emptor*, 10, November/December 1973, pp. 14–15, 23.

—— "Review of *The Mothman Prophecies*." *Fate*, November 1975, p. 107.

Goerman, Robert A. "Mothmania." *Fate*, June 2001: 8–12.

Hall, Mark A. "Bighoot—The Giant Owl." *Wonders*, 5,3, September 1998, pp. 67–79.

Keel, John A. *The Fickle Finger of Fate*. Greenwich, Connecticut: Fawcett, 1966 (novel).

—— "North America 1966: Development of a Great Wave." *Flying Saucer Review*. 13,2, March/April1967, pp. 3–9.

—— "From My Ohio Valley Note Book." *Flying Saucer Review*. 13,3, May/June 1967, pp. 3–5.

—— "UFO 'Agents of Terror'." *Saga*. October 1967, pp. 29–31,72–74,76–79,81.

—— "UFO Report: The Sinister Men in Black." *Fate*. 21,4, April 1968. pp. 32–39.

—— "A New Approach to UFO Witnesses." *Flying Saucer Review*. 14,3, May/June 1968, pp. 7–14.

—— "West Virginia's Enigmatic 'Bird'." *Flying Saucer Review*. 14,4, July/August 1968, pp. 7–14.

—— "Mothman Monster," *Saga,* 37,1, October 1968, pp. 66–70.

—— "Is the 'EM' Effect a Myth?" *Flying Saucer Review*. 14,6, November/December 1968, pp. 16–18.

—— *The Telephone Problem in the United States*. New York: The Author, 1968.

—— "The Time Cycle Factor." *Flying Saucer Review*. 15,3, May/June 1969, pp. 9–13.

—— "MIB: 1967–1968." *Saucer News*. 16,4, Spring/Summer 1969, pp. 5–6.

—— "The Principle of Transmogrification." *Flying Saucer Review*. 15,4. July/August 1969. pp. 27–28,31.

—— "The 'Superior' Technology: Some Generalities." *Flying Saucer Review*. 15,5, September/October 1969, pp. 26–27,29.

—— "Fables of the UFO Age." *Fate*. 23,8, August 1970, pp. 90, 94,96.

—— *UFOs: Operation Trojan Horse*. New York: G. P. Putnam's Sons, 1970.

—— *Strange Creatures from Time and Space*. Greenwich, CT: Fawcett Gold Medal, 1970.

—— *Operation Trojan Horse: An Exhaustive Study of Unidentified Flying Objects—Revealing Their Source and the Forces That Control Them*. London: Souvenir Press, 1971

—— *Our Haunted Planet: Mysteries of Time and Space*. N.Y.: Fawcett, 1971.

—— *The Mothman Prophecies. An Investigation into the Mysterious American Visits of the Infamous Feathery Garuda*. N.Y: Saturday Review Press, E.P. Dutton & Co., Inc., 1975.

—— *The Mothman Prophecies,* NY: Signet, 1975.

—— *Strange Creatures from Time & Space.* London: Neville Spearman, 1975.

—— "The Flying Saucer Subculture." *Journal of Popular Culture.* 8, 1975: 871–96.

—— *The Eighth Tower* N.Y: Saturday Review Press, E.P. Dutton & Co., Inc., 1975.

—— *Visitors from Space: The Astonishing, True Story of the Mothman Prophecies.* London: Panther, 1976.

—— *The Cosmic Question: Man and the Supernatural—A Stunning New Perspective (The Eighth Tower* in USA). Herts, UK: Panther, 1978.

—— "UFOs, Mothman and Me: Twenty Years on the Flying Saucer Beat." *High Times.* 57, May 1980, pp. 42–45,72–75.

—— *Disneyland of the Gods: An Investigation into Psychic Phenomena and the Outer Limits of Human Perception.* New York: Amok Press, 1988.

—— *The Mothman Prophecies*, Lilburn, GA: IllumiNet Press, 1991.

—— *The Mothman.* NY: New York Fortean Society, 1991 Pamplet, 6 pp.

—— "Beyond the Known: Mothman," *Fate,* March 1991, pp. 21–22.

—— *The Complete Guide To Mysterious Beings*, New York, New York: Bantam Doubleday Dell Publishing Group, 1994.

—— *Disneyland of the Gods.* Lilburn, Georgia: IllumiNet Press, 1995.

—— *The Mothman Prophecies.* NY: Tor, 2002 edition.

Keith, Jim. "MIBs in a Test Tube," in *Casebook on the Men in Black.* Lilburn, GA: IllumiNet Press, 1997, pp. 126–141.

Miller, Virginia Margaret. "Report from the Readers: The 'Mothman' Visits." *Fate* 29,3, March 1976, pp. 127–129.

Moseley, James W. "Offbeat: Mothman." *Real Magazine,* August 1967, p. 23.

—— "West Virginia 'Moth Man' Terrorizes Many," *Saucer News,* Spring 1967, pp. 35–36.

—— "Mysterious 'Moth Man' Sightings Continue in West Virginia," *Saucer News,* Summer 1967, pp. 24–25.

Mozier, Jeanne. *Way out in West Virginia: A Must-Have Guide to the Oddities and Wonders of the Mountain State.* Charleston, WV: Quarrier Press, 1999.

North, E. Lee. *Redcoats, Redskins and Red-Eyed Monsters.* New York: A. S. Barnes, 1979.

Raynes, Brent and Ron Schaffner. "West Virginia Revisited." *Ohio Sky Watcher.* January/February/March 1976, pp. 9–10.

Sergent Jr, Donnie and Jeff Wamsley. *Mothman: The Facts Behind The Legend.* Point Pleasant, WV: Mothmanlives Productions, 2001.

Sharp, Alan W. "Do You Know John Keel?" *Merseyside UFO Bulletin* 4,3, Summer 1971, pp. 32–35.

Teets, Bob. "Of Monsters, Ships & Giant Birds?" and "Another Mothman Sighting?" *West Virginia UFOs: Close Encounters in the Mountain State* Terra Alta, WV: Headline Books, 1994.

Thomas, Kenneth. "Winged Cats, Mothman and Unidentified Flying Objects," in *Popular Alienation*, Lilburn, GA: IllumiNet Press, 1996, pp. 129–130
White, Helen. "Do Birds Come This Big?" *Fate*, August 1967, pp. 74–77.

Mothman Websites

1. The Mothman Lives
Presents accounts of Mothman sightings, news on the movie *The Mothman Prophecies* and a discussion forum devoted to this glowing-eyed creature. Has information on Donnie Sergent, Jr.'s "Mothman: The Facts Behind the Legend" CD-ROM.
http://www.mothmanlives.com

2. Mothman—Ghosts of the Prairie
Recounts the strange sighting in Point Pleasant of a giant, moth-like creature. Includes a composite sketch and recommended reading.
http://www.prairieghosts.com/moth.html

3. Blather Archives: A Mothman Retrospective
Having finally read the previously neglected copy of John Keel's 1975 Fortean classic *The Mothman Prophecies*, Blather shares their insights.
http://www.blather.net/archives2/issue2no5.html

4. Mothman—The Cryptozoo
Recounts the unexplained sighting in Point Pleasant, West Virginia, of a large, winged creature with glowing red eyes.
http://www.parascope.com/en/cryptozoo/predators02.htm

5. Mystery of Mothman Revisited
General review of the Mothman events.
http://www.geocities.com/SunsetStrip/Alley/7982/mothman.htm

6. Point Pleasant, West Virginia
Learn more about the location of the Mothman events.
http://webpages.marshall.edu/~irby1/pleasant.html

7. Mothman Prophecies
An attractive, easy to navigate site on everything from the new books and movies to "The Detour," the Mothman episode of the "X-Files."
http://www.mothman-prophecies.com

Mothman Filmography

Special Investigations: Mothman. Tom L Byron, director. Also known as: *Mothman: The Point Pleasant Phenomenon.* Bryon Productions, 1996 (docudrama).

Mothman. Douglas TenNapel, director. Mr. Black Production, 2000 (fiction film).

Search for the Mothman. David Grabias, director. Sinema/Sony, 2002 (documentary).

Mothman Prophecies, The. Mark Pellington, director. Screen Gems/Sony, 2002 (fiction film).

Mothman Memorabilia

Nevermore Creations has a "Legendary Monsters" Mothman (5 inches tall) figure, with a victim figure, based on Linda Scarberry, and a descriptive card on the sighting. R. Todd Broadwater, Westmont, New Jersey, is the Director of Product Development. 2001-2002.
http://www.legendarymonsters.com/
http://www.toymania.com/news/messages/1093.shtml

The Great Mystery Museum Collection has a small (2.5 inches) action Mothman figure, direct from Japan, 2001.
http://www.geocities.com/gordonrutter/myst.html

Mezco Toys has an insectlike Mothman figure (5 inches tall), 2001.
www.mezco.net/crypto.html

Acknowledgments

The stimulation for this book came out of discussions I had with Patrick Huyghe, friend and editor-in-chief of Paraview Books. I wish to express my gratitude to him for his continued encouragement of this project, one I have been interested in doing for years. Needless to say, John A. Keel's help along the way is deeply appreciated, from his long, cryptic letters in the 1960s to our likewise lengthy talks in 2001. Thank you, John, for going to Point Pleasant, and bringing back so much that is captured in that one spooky phrase "Mothman."

Direct time and support for this book came from Leslie, Malcolm, and Caleb. My thanks is a minor act compared to all you did for me; it is an understatement to say I could not have done this without you.

Jerome Clark's and my old material merged and separated in various chapters on winged weirdies, black dogs, and more. This input was essential; thank you, Jerry. A special Fortean appreciation is noted for Mark A. Hall, who continues to be supportive with advice and information, and was especially insightful with theories on giant owls and merbeings. Other building blocks came through the generous help of George Eberhart, Phyllis Galde, Robert Goerman, Terry W. Colvin, Troy Taylor, Bob Rickard, Rod Dyke, Mark Pilkington, Richard Hendricks, Bill Rebsamen, Harry Trumbore, Linda Godfrey, R. Todd Broadwater, Gordon Rutter, Rich La Monica, David Grabias, Kenn Thomas, Donnie Sergent Jr., Todd Roll, S. Miles Lewis, Michael Newton, Daniel Cohen, Craig Heinselman, Betty Hill, Rik Billock, Gilbert Miller, Des Miller, Mike Oxbig, Ray Nelke, Burt Warmeister, Sara Garrett, Stan Gordon, Louise A. Lowry, Matt Drudge, Uri Geller, Whitney Strieber, Libbet Cone, Amy Hayes, Ron Schaffner, Scott Corrales, Jon Downes, Blake Mathys, David Bittner, Darren Naish, Paul Herman, Dan Porter, T. Peter Park, Lisa Stone, Craig Woolheater, Brad Steiger, Curt Sutherly, Chad Arment, Rick Noll, Rob Riggs, Jim Boyd, and Bob Hieronimus. Special thanks to Bill Rebsamen, the cover artist and illustrator, and Laura Smyth, the cover and layout designer, for their tireless creative treatments. Also, a tip of my hat to

Marc Weinstock, vice-president of marketing at Sony/Screen Gems, for his thought-provoking questions about my interest in Mothman.

There are literally hundreds of email correspondents, individuals, organizations, and publications who have helped me down through the years, some of whom I mentioned under this heading in *Mysterious America*. All of those folks have assisted directly or indirectly in bringing about this book, too. My investigations and the phenomena merge from one to the next, and these friends were along on this Mothman journey as well. Thank you all.

Loren Coleman
PO Box 360
Portland, Maine 04112
mothman@lorencoleman.com
www.lorencoleman.com
12.24.01

Index

This index avoids recording every appearance of the words "Mothman," "Point Pleasant," and "West Virginia," as these are found throughout the text. The appendices and bibliography are not indexed, as these sections allow for easy access to their contents.